MW00512742

Image Bearer

A Message To
A Younger Me

Image Bearer

A Message To
A Younger Me

EXECUTIVE EDITOR
DR. TUESDAY TATE

PUBLISHING

Copyright 2020 Dr. Tuesday Tate

All rights reserved. This book is protected by the copyright laws of the United States of America. This book, its' contents and or cover may not be copied or reprinted for in whole or in part, stored in a retrieval system or transmitted to any form or by any means: electronic, mechanical, photocopy, recording or any other for any commercial gain or profit. The use of short quotations, occasional page copying for personal or group study or the contributing author using their chapter only is permitted.

Published by
ATK PUBLISHING
8401 Moller Rd. Ste. 68244
Indianapolis, IN 46268
www.atkspf.com
www.drtuesday.net

Image Bearers | A Message to a Younger Me

ISBN 978-1-7324174-5-8

Printed in the United States of America

Library of Congress Control Number
2019912322

Editing by:
Nataph Consulting

Cover design by:
Tracy Denmark

CONTENTS

DEDICATION

This book is dedicated to every pre-teen, teen, in-between teen, and young woman who we once were. Own and walk in the image and likeness of God's beauty and magnificence. HE created, formed, and fashioned you to be unique. No need to be a copycat or envy another. You are an original. Like you; love you! Nobody can be or do you better than you. Be great at being you. If you don't, who will? The world is waiting on you to show up. I present to you the amazing and wonderful <your name>! Boldly, confidently, graciously, beautifully, and humbly bear the image and likeness of God. You are His workmanship. Created in and by Him to be spectacular! I give you permission to go for it and just do it!

INTRODUCTION

Every earthly father provides the seed that determines our unique makeup and our mother provides the incubator to house and protect us until it is time for us to come into the world. And now, here we are – their child! Have you ever looked at your parent or parents and saw yourself? Or maybe at one stage of your life, you looked like your mom and another your dad? More amazing is when you looked at him or her and thought "I don't see either one of them when I look in the mirror."

Who do I resemble? People will say, "Oh, you look just like your dad (at that age) or you look like your mom." "Ok, thank you, but I don't see it. What are they seeing? The image I see looking back at me is not the same as my father or mother." Well, beloved, I have your answer. Though your mom and dad came together to conceive you, it was God who created and formed you in His image (Genesis 1:27). And that image is love and beauty! Like Christ, you are an Image Bearer of God. You were formed to graciously bear (wear, taken on) His image.

In a "Focus on the Family" article titled "What It Means to Be *Made in the Image of God"* it says, "As believers in Christ, we have a "new self, which is renewed in knowledge after the image of its creator" (Colossians 3:10). As we grow in faith, we "are being transformed into God's image from one degree of glory to another" (2nd Corinthians 3:18). Knowing that we are made in God's image should positively affect our understanding of God, our relationship with Him, our love for Him and ourselves, and our respect for others. It should also set the stage for understanding and defending the sanctity of *ALL* human life.

From the beginning of time to the establishing of the United States, being created in the God-image is a truth that was considered, stated, and documented. Therefore, it cannot be denied or debunked. The Declaration of Independence (DOI) puts it like this, *"**WE** hold these Truths to be self-evident (obvious), that ALL Men* (human beings) *are created equal, and they are endowed by their Creator* (and that Creator is God)..." Even God's Word that came before the DOI gave way to this declaration and validates its purpose and truth. We find in Romans 2:11 and Acts 10:34 that "God shows no partiality (no arbitrary favoritism; with Him one person is not more important than another); HE is not a respecter of person." When we do not accept, respect, and apply this truth, we as human beings and specifically Christians are rejecting God as the Creator and His creation (yourself). These eight contributing Authors have accepted and applied this truth.

Psalm 139:13-14 is one of the most recognized scriptures that speaks to the beauty of God's choice to create us. It reminds us that God created us fearfully and wonderfully! What does that mean? In this scripture, fearfully is defined as marvelously and awesomely. For over 25 years, this was the message I sought to communicate to my mentees in the Indianapolis Public Middle and High Schools, Girl Scouts, Girls Inc., my Church, and as a Chaplin in the juvenile center. These authors coming together to share their fearfully made stories in this publication have brought a 20-year-old vision to fruition.

Image Bearer brings to life the above scripture and speaks to the fact and truth that we were all created in God's image. That image is love, goodness, awesomeness and so much more! Consider this, everything about God is great that is what you were created from. Yet, somewhere along the way, the truth (that we were, and are, fearfully and wonderfully made in the image of God) was lost in translation, application, and or it was never articulated or instilled. Because of the distortion of the media, the lies of our experiences, environment, and our emotional need for approval and acceptance, we – particularly females, lose our way! Well, this inspiring book is for you. It is for any and all women who in the past or present struggle with their shade color, size/weight, identity, the need for love, African-American features, acceptance, your worth and value, talent, ability, etc.

We hope you see your uniqueness and beauty and celebrate how far you have come! Though, I am confident these stories will inspire, encourage, and bless every woman who reads them, it is written specifically for 'Gen Z' (teens to 29 year-olds). It speaks to the struggle of when we were teens and younger women! You will laugh, cry, be angry, shout, be shocked, and praise God for their (and know your) victory! Each author writes a letter to her younger self, encouraging her to focus on her exceptional future that is to come! The letters alone will inspire.

Just as God allowed our great-grandparents to come together to get our grandparents here, they came together to get our parents here, and our parents came together for the sole purpose of getting you and me here. Why? Because

God had a grand purpose and plan for us and our lives. And as with all human beings, we were created in His image. Thus, with all things HE formed, fashioned, and brought forth, HE said you and I were very good (Genesis 1:31) and declared we are marvelous and wonderful.

Now that you have this knowledge, truth, and understanding, let's talk about why many of us find it difficult to accept and apply this as young girls and women. First, understand that God makes no mistakes. HE created you and formed you because HE loved you before your mom or dad knew you. Remember, "*God so loved the world* (and that includes you) *that HE gave His only begotten Son (Jesus)...(John 3:16)."* You being born, having a life and purpose was not a "mishap" of God's. As His creation, HE has declared that you are awesome, beautiful, and wonderful. Say it with me, "I am loved and I have a purpose!" Believe it and believe Him; accept it, rest in it, and walk in it. You are God's beautiful workmanship, His prize creation that HE calls His beloved and His daughter. You are the apple of His eye.

Rachel A. Wright

Rachel was born in Chicago, IL, and currently resides in Indianapolis, IN. She is the mother of two gracefully-blooming daughters, Meorah, 13, and Mazyrah, 5. Although mothering is her most prized responsibility, Rachel wears a plethora of hats: graphic designer by trade, prophetic orator, preacher, teacher, biblical advisor, youth leader, rapper, and an author! Since 2011, she has helped build the local church. She has obtained formal education in business and administration, and leadership at IUPUI and Ivy Tech. Her life's ambition is to help people reconnect with a healthy self-awareness and understand their true identity and purpose from the perspective of their Maker.

From Stud to Stunning
~by Rachel A. Wright~

Introduction: An Encounter with God

I vividly remember, around the tender age of five having what I have grown to understand as a "God-encounter." "Jesus, Jeeee-suuss," I melodically sang a song that my heart had spontaneously written as I joyfully leaped from couch to couch in my mom's stylish living room. The thick peace that consumed that room was indescribable.

At that moment, I was too young to know how to appreciate such a rich, full experience. After all, a heart of bliss was typical at a young age. However, the enemy of my soul always hated that spark of joy, that resilient fire that violently burned within me. This joy was constantly fanning a flame of strength. Now looking back, as far as I can remember, I see how the enemy has always aspired to suffocate that fire and, in turn, stifle me. It is these types of memories that have reinforced my confidence in who God is and has been in my life and who He created me to be. As I spiritually matured, the Lord gradually opened my eyes. I now recognize that I have had countless instances of "God-encounters." The Spirit of God has graced me to understand that it was the fire of God that preserved me through the battles of my life.

The fire of God works two ways: it engulfs and protects us, and it destroys all that is unlike Him - all at the same time! I know it may be difficult to understand, but it will make sense later. It is my great pleasure to say that I survived and lived through an alternative lifestyle. I escaped from the grisly grips of Hell's rage by the power of God. He allowed me to make a comeback so I could expose the tactics of dark, unseen forces, and satanic agents. The kingdom of darkness attempted to use the powers of perversion and homosexuality to destroy what God had in store for me. It sought to dismantle my purpose, destiny, and ultimately me!

Origin of Identity: The Source of Purpose

Seeking answers to their identity crisis, many people navigate through this life, searching for the very essence of who they are. They rely on millions of hits per second from Google and Siri: w*hat is my purpose; where are my roots, who are my ancestors, and why am I here?* While this generation believes that search engines and genealogy sites are the ultimate authority for discovering their purpose, there is an ancient authority that existed far beyond today's technology. He is the *Only* Wise God, The Almighty One, The Ancient of Days, The Father of Creation! It is in, and by, His boundless wisdom that I have found the answers to countless questions concerning my life.

The first chapter of James urges us to ask God for wisdom if we lack any and without restraint, He will generously grant our requests. The Spirit of Wisdom leads to the understanding of all things, and when you sincerely seek Him, He will guide you to all truth.

Jeremiah 1:5 declares, *"Before I formed you in the womb I knew you [and approved of you as My chosen instrument], and before you were born I consecrated you [to Myself as My own];I have appointed you as a prophet to the nations"* (AMP). Now, let us break this down. God declared that before I was a sperm cell, driven from the fertile loins of my father, taking up nine months residence in my mom's womb, the Creator of *all* flesh thoroughly knew and understood everything concerning me. He fully embraced and endorsed me as His own, the cream of the crop, preferred, and chosen to be His great delight! The Lord God considered me as His sacred treasure.

Before releasing me into the earth through the bowels of my mother, He officially authorized me as one of Heaven's ambassadors. To put it plainly, we were first conceived in the mind of God, created in the womb of woman, and chosen by the God of Heaven to display His glory in the earth! God devised our purpose *before* conception, while Satan planned your demise at birth. Since we arrived on earth, Heaven and Hell have been and are at war for our souls!

You are a masterpiece, endorsed, and sculpted by the hands of a mastermind! For this reason, at times, you have felt the blazing heat of the battle between good and evil forces in your life. As I shine the light on some life events, I can see how the forces of good and evil wrestled for the possession of my soul. Perhaps you too will be enlightened and able to see how God, in His perfect wisdom has been using every significant event in your life to awaken you to His enduring presence. His hope has always been to draw you closer to His heart and your purpose by the power of His untainted love. Likewise, Satan has been working behind the scenes to use those same life events to draw you away from the heart, mind, and purpose of God.

Groundwork: The Foundation of Family

God does nothing without pure intentions. Everything that we see on earth was intended to mirror the image of God and reveal how He and the Kingdom of Heaven functions. God literally wants you to experience heaven on earth, but deception has persuaded many to dismiss this idea as an overly used cliché', rather than embracing it as an attainable reality that is accessible through our full obedience and submission to the Lord.

Hosea 4:6 declares that we are destroyed because of a lack of knowledge. For too long, we have rejected the knowledge and understanding of God's way of doing things. Insomuch, the whole world is now experiencing the consequences of the blatant disregard for what God requires from us as His children.

Due to our ignorance of who God is, and what He expects from us as a Father, the enemy has taken advantage of us and has used our freewill, ignorance, and willful rebellion towards God to backfire and, undoubtedly, destroy the mind, spirit, and soul of man. However, once we as a people awaken to the understanding of God's good intents, and the satisfying purpose that He has for our lives, we will no longer fall victim to spiritual burglary and the hijacking of our souls.

This culture has failed miserably in its attempts to redefine family.

This constant cycle of ignorance and rebellion has left many of us blind to the manipulative, persuasive stratagems of the enemy, and has ultimately affected our homes, communities, and nation in undesirable ways. This culture has failed miserably in its attempt to redefine family. Seeing that God is the original creator and authority of the idea of family, His blueprint and careful instructions are without flaw. Neither are the guidelines by which He has defined "family" are not up for debate or discussion.

We honor every other founding company and their creative authority on how to use, care for, and identify what is considered the proper use and function of their working or malfunctioning product. Yet, when it comes to God, the creator of all things (human, animal, or plant life), we disregard His authority and instructions on how it and we are to live (function). If we would only return to the Manufacturer (God) and allow Him to restore us, marriages, and family back to their originally intended purpose and function; how amazing we would be?

God had the power of love in mind when He established the institution of the family! Through the family, God displays His glory by putting His characteristics and nature on display for the whole world to see. In the institution of family, the man is the demonstrated love and strength of God; woman, the manifested wisdom and kindness of God, and children are to be the revealed gentleness and humility of God. When these traits are harmoniously intertwined, you get a vivid depiction of who God is in His fullness. The displaying of His glory for all of creation to see! Hallelujah! Talk about relationship goals! The family has power over evil and a strong influence on the earth, bringing praise-worthy credit back to the Creator!

Unfortunately, the enemy has successfully displaced or removed every member of the family from its proper position, distorting the trustworthiness of God by demolishing the family structure with his deceptive methods. He does this by playing the pain card. Now, instead of displaying men with a strong, and bold spirit of leadership and guidance, we are, often, sold the narrative of weakened, discouraged, lazy, violent, incompetent angry men suffering from all forms of overindulgence, stress, and distress; resulting in confusion and rage.

Our women are, often, portrayed as vain, foolish, angry, and hostile rather than one who is full of life-altering wisdom and beauty, inside and out, having the potential to change the course of nations through understanding and shifting the hearts of many back to the Father! Consequently, many of our children are given over to grief, pride, sexual perversion, and rebellion, causing an abundance of destruction and premature deaths!

We desperately need to get back to obeying the order and guidelines of God, starting with the family! Our families, and communities, are broken because we have failed to carefully follow the bible, which the original manufacturer of our souls has provided! The wisdom found in this "manual" is far beyond what any man could imagine. I have found out for myself that its contents are life-changing when applied and practiced in everyday life! With all the chaos in this world, it's time that we utilize the transforming power of the Word of God, by obeying. At this point, what do we have to lose?

Before releasing me to face this merciless world, my first line of defense, my parents, failed to impart solid wisdom and good examples into my life and me. With this understanding, it is no surprise that I had become exposed to so much misleading and deception, leaving me vulnerable to spiritual, mental, and emotional larceny at an early age. Like an overwhelming sum of prior generations, I was not exposed to a stable home environment.

My home was never that comprised of both a god-fearing, steadfast father and a praying, wisdom-filled mother. Though I was robbed of the opportunity to, potentially, have the influence of my father in my life, due to his death (I'll go into that a little later), my mother didn't intentionally labor to fully equip me with the wisdom of God; to overthrow the dictates and temptations of this troubled world.

Hell had hijacked God's purpose for the family, including mine, leaving many oblivious to their identity. Society and my environment consisted of those broken families, wounded, and scarred with grief. Too many families have released their children as marred pillars into society, inadequately built to uphold cultural, community, or family standards that align with the ways of God. This family structure breakdown has left a generation devoid of discovering their identity and living in and through the strength of God.

The lack of wholeness nurtured in the home has produced an army of young people seeking for that solid ground of love, peace, and purpose in all the wrong places. In Genesis chapter one, God gave us dominion to rule the earth He created: to govern His creation and to firmly stand on and enforce His laws on earth. But sadly, His children (those who have confessed His Son as Savior and Lord) do not realize He's given us the world to rule (Psalm 115:16) and take dominion (control) over. Understand, if the foundation of a thing is built poorly, the need for reconstruction is guaranteed.

The Seed

One of God's objectives for the family that comes by marriage is to produce and multiply a *righteous* seed. According to Malachi 2, one of the objectives of a Godly union (marriage) is to nurture the seed (child) through the teachings of God and His Word. God is wise and thoughtful, establishing all things with good intentions, including an unbelievable plan in store for every one of us who has accepted His Son as Savior and Lord. See, God loves order, and He dwells therein. Remember how I referred to God designing the family?

The guidelines for establishing and keeping a family are in Genesis 1 and 3. It was for our protection and growth both on the earth and in God. Unfortunately, society has disregarded Godly wisdom to establish their idea of the right way of doing things (Romans 10:3). Our intentions, apart from Godly wisdom, bring hardships to ourselves and to those who are subject to us. That's why it's called *Holy* matrimony. The design was for two people, man, and woman, who love and obey the Lord, and honor and respect Him and each other. Anything outside of this is guaranteed to face challenges and penalties that God never intended for Holy Matrimony.

Marriage is an earthly replica of Christ and the Church. God declares in His Word that the husband ought to love his wife like Christ loved the Church (Ephesians 5:25). Conception and childbirth through fornication (outside of the marriage covenant) was never the way of God. Yes, the child is a blessing, according to Psalm 127:3, but the act of producing children outside of marriage is sin. Fornication is rooted in lust, and any relationship built on lustfulness is bound to result in confusion, heartbreak, and brokenness.

I believe God spends an overwhelming amount of time trying to save us from the error of our ways. I'm convinced that He would rather be blessing us beyond our wildest imaginations. If only we would fully commit to and obey His commands! The Bible tells us that the commandments of God are not agonizing (1 John 5:3). The enemy has tricked us into thinking that following the ways and commandments of God is boring, and burdensome, and doing things our way is okay. But both could not be further from the truth. I have personally witnessed the remarkable happiness and peace that comes with following God!

There are so many biblical accounts revealing the mind of God, supporting His idea for family. First of all, family begins with a man because the seed is in the man. God has designated man to be head of the family unit, ultimately giving him the responsibility to guard, guide, and grow the members of his household. Secondly, he should be a man sufficiently acquainted with the Lord and His Spirit, equipped with wisdom to lead, build, steer, and counsel his family.

He must understand that he can't effectively fulfill these God-given responsibilities without the Lord's help. It's about time we raise and train our sons to understand that starting a family should be a God-led decision and an honor to do so. Man's obedience to God and commitment to his family would eliminate a massive amount of chaos and confusion that the family structure is experiencing today. It's vital that a man has a strong relationship with Jesus and makes Him his head (1 Cor. 11:3).

This spiritual relationship is ideal before he considers finding a wife and starting a family. The man is the representation of God in and over the family in the earth: not to lord over, but to love, protect, provide, and instruct. Malachi, chapter two, warns man that he should maintain a spirit of faithfulness to his wife. It goes on to say that God hates divorce; so, he should check his spirit self to make sure being faithful to his wife and family is a trait he is committed to keeping.

Now, this accounts for what *should* be the case, but we all know this isn't always the reality. That's where the grace of God comes in to fill the void of every dark hole and desire in our lives where lack of discipline resides! This level of commitment is significant and necessary to nurturing the mother and carrying of the father's seed through conception, labor, delivery, and life on this side of the womb.

Every seed carries and produces its kind. For example, if it's an apple seed, you'll get apples; if it's an orange seed, you'll get oranges, and so on. We are all seeds of a man; planted in the soil of our mother's womb. It is from his seed that our gender is determined. With that said, not only do genetics produce attributes that are physical traits of our mothers and fathers, but studies also support the idea that genetics plays a role in influencing our personality and behavior traits.

Have you ever asked yourself, "Why am I like this?" Well, my friend, I think few will argue with the belief that we are an intertwined makeup of our mother and father's DNA! Eventually, I realized that the seed and its DNA go beyond the physical. It is also spiritual and is called generational curses, and they are indeed real!

Some of the dysfunctional ways I struggled with were associated with my bloodline; physical, environmental, and spiritual. I had to understand that the battle didn't start with me, nor was it mine alone. But I soon learned though it was not my fault, it was my fight! It was bigger than me. It was generational, spiritual confrontations with spirits that existed in the bloodlines of both my father and mother. These spirits knew which bloodline I belonged to and took the initiative to hunt me down.

Very few men and women consider the lasting spiritual consequences that come with their lack of self-restraint in the moment of time and lust. The actions of an undisciplined man planting his seed in the thorn-riddled field of a heart-broken insecure woman's womb can prove to be spiritually, mentally, and emotionally dangerous for the seed – the child in the end. The environment (the womb) in which he plants his seed will affect if it lives, how it grows, and develops.

Nature vs. Nurture

After several centuries, it traces back as far as the 4th century, the classic ongoing debate of nature vs. nurture, and its concept, still carries controversial weight in the world of psychology. The nature vs. nurture argument analyzes whether human behavior is influenced by genetics or by the environment. Both nature and nurture are evaluated through a scientific branch of study known as Behavioral Genetics. Nature explores how genetic inheritance and other biological factors play a role in influencing one's behaviors.

Whereas nurture concentrates on how external factors, such as life experiences, environment, and learned behavior, contribute to the shaping of one's conduct. While both stand on opposing sides, assertively arguing their case, I take a firm stance to offer an alternative perspective. I believe that both genetic and environmental factors work hand-in-hand in shaping our behavior. I'm convinced that you cannot have one without the other. Whatever's released through us by speech and temperament creates an environment. Our environments are direct results of what comes out of those that occupy that space.

For example, it is required for daycares to create a safe learning environment. With that, there are certain acceptable behaviors and tolerated speech that is required to create a suitable environment that produces productive learning and safety.

Simply put, whatever is in you (genetics) will eventually spill over into your atmosphere (environment) conducive to encouraging other behaviors. Just follow me, we are going on a spiritual journey.

The Spirit of the Orphan

I think childhood is the closest we are to the state of God before life introduces us to corruption. Scripture says that God is love, and there is no creature more loving than a child. I believe that children are the epitome of unconditional, unrestricted love. The deep desire to love, be loved and have a sense of belonging begins at childhood. If that craving isn't satisfied early, many will pursue all types of counterfeit affections to fill a void in their adulthood. It is their pain that eventually seeks pleasure.

Those who suffer from feelings of abandonment, rejection, and neglect try to numb that deep internal pain through various types of physical, emotional, mental, and sexual stimuli. Some try to medicate their heartache with toxic relationships, money, fame, and their idea of success, drug abuse, alcohol consumption, self-mutilation, tattoos, piercings, unclean humor, and an unending list of unhealthy motivations. Only the presence of God can heal an abandoned and broken spirit. The orphan spirit is often related to being wounded by someone in a position of authority, usually tracing back to a childhood experience(s).

Some occurrence associated with trauma, abandonment, neglect, or rejection has transpired and left a deep wound on the soul and spirit. Someone suffering from the Orphan Spirit sees life through the filter of abandonment, neglect, rejection, rage, etc. Their expression of this spiritual condition varies; some display the effects of this condition through pride, anger, rebellion, and coldness, while others exhibit symptoms of depression, loneliness, insecurity, and fear.

Those who are affected and infected with the orphan spirit have a constant need for continued reassurance that others will love them and stay with them. Though you cannot cast out an orphan spirit, you can be delivered and healed from it. It is a result of ungodly beliefs and attitudes that have developed over your lifetime, through emotional pressures and mental afflictions. Word curses spoken over your life, and exposure to certain behaviors, lifestyles, and environments can mold specific attitudes.

Life experiences have conditioned the mind to take on a stance and defensive mechanism that becomes a part of your personality, character, and emotional makeup. It is the reason you respond, act, and live the way you do in private, before God, and others. It's a mentality. It's a mindset that has shaped your spirit and leads your body to follow suit.

Proverbs 23:7 says, as an individual thinks in his heart, so is he. You, in your current state, are the way you are because of the things you've seen and endured, and for some, it's because of how you've allowed this way of thinking to influence you, your life, and relationships. Be encouraged, the wise counsel of God has the power to shift your perspective and your view of life. You can and will see through a clear lens. I am so glad our circumstances don't have the last say-so in who we will become.

My Upbringing

I was never given the childhood pleasure of proudly relishing in the whole 'how mom and dad met' tidbit. I had heard some stories from a family source on my mother's side, but the accounts were not at all tasteful. Although some of them were believable, I could not verify the accuracy of the stories, so I just left it at that for the time being. Anytime I would ask my mom about my dad, she seemed to have always been under the power of some sinister presence, padlocking her jaws shut, escaping the question through a fit of rage and rebuttal!

Her reaction always raised a red flag of concern for me. The older I grew, the stronger her rejection was toward me. It led me to believe that she had resentment toward my dad. It became clear that her response had absolutely nothing to do with me.

Ultimately, I've used the power of my imagination to create a narrative of how my parents potentially met and united. If I could describe my mother in one word, it would be 'vulnerable;' thus, my name choice is Mara, which means bitter. Many people are attracted to one another for a multitude of reasons, some good and some bad. So, pinpointing what their exact attraction was towards each other is almost impossible.

Unfortunately, or maybe not, I never had the chance to meet my father, whom I will call Thann, which means death or brilliant. I had some small, informal introductions to him through information from other members on his side of the family. Perhaps, maybe, he had an irresistible charm that mom couldn't shake, as family sources had previously made mention to me about his stellar athleticism. If my calculations serve me correctly, I believe it was likely a cold winter night in January of 1985. The streets were alive with rambunctious city crawlers and lightweight traffic, racing through the dark streets.

The moonlight lit up the Chicago night with its semi-full face and shimmering brilliance, and the heat of the moment surpassed the evening's winter chill. Not long after, seduction drew Thann and Mara closer together, and they conceived a baby girl. Sadly, about seven months into Mara's pregnancy, Thann was murdered, and in the Fall season, on October 6th, Mara was faced with the harsh reality of giving birth to and raising her baby girl, Rachel A. Wright, all alone.

My upbringing was pretty predictable for a baby growing up in America in the '80s; living in a single parent home with my mother. With little to no help, she daily faced the pressures of raising children alone. She juggled home responsibilities and pursued employment stable enough to satisfy her desire to provide for her children the things she had never had. Not to mention, wrestling to keep her sanity intact posed to be quite strenuous! Most children do not have the rational aptitude to comprehend the mental, spiritual, and emotional vulnerabilities that comes with taking on such demanding obligations, but boy, do I get it now!

Society highlights the ugly marks carved on the heart of a child, resulting from absentee fathers. But rarely is the other side of the coin examined: the unattractive marks left by a mother. I believe the effects of an emotionally absent and dysfunctional mother are just as catastrophic to a child as that of a negligent father. A child's need for healthy emotional management and spiritual training (Proverbs 22:6) is vital for proper development into adulthood. Psalm 27:10 says, "W*hen my father* and my *mother forsake me*, then the Lord will take me up."

Though my home environment was compromised by spiritual and emotional negligence, the Lord's grace proved to be sufficient to protect and build me up where parental guidance had failed. I'm so glad the power of God is not hindered by life's hurdles, nor restricted by our limitations and weaknesses. For when we are weak, He shows Himself mighty and strong in us (2 Cor. 12:9)! Parents and guardians set the tone for their children's future. Whether good or bad, often the standards they live by leave a lasting impression on their children, affecting them into adulthood.

...love didn't live in my mom's heart consistently.

Abuse defined is the mishandling or misuse of something or someone. I recall my mother being subject to different forms of violence and abuse: drug, mental, verbal, and emotional abuse from numerous partners. We all know there is a right and wrong way to handle people. When I was growing up, a healthy dose of affection was not displayed anywhere in my life. There were no hugs and kisses, something children, and people of all ages, desperately need but may never admit. I don't remember hearing many, "I love you's." Why is that...? Because love didn't *live* in my mom's heart consistently.

There was always an emotional disconnect between my mother and me. I can count on one hand how many times we laughed together. Financial lack was a painful reality, too. Although I was exceptionally talented and smart, the addiction robbed our home of the financial investments and resources needed to nurture and develop my gifts. I had an athletic skill that was second to none, likely accredited to my father's sporty ability. I can only imagine where I would've ended up had my mother invested in, guarded, and nurtured the gifts and talents within me.

Emotional neglect and financial suppression served to be the hardest blows that damaged me the most. These challenges ultimately led me to have a bitter heart. Sadly, at a young age, I developed a soul of armor. This hardened soul set me up to journey down a cold dark road of deep pits, tremendous pain, and great rage. No, this is not new. Satan has used pain to blind and distort the perception of mankind since the beginning of time.

We must learn how to channel our pain healthily, using it to our advantage and not towards our demise. Today, I place no blame on my mother because I get the bigger picture now. As I matured, I came to understand that whatever mistreatment she was exposed to, in her earlier years connected to me and leaked into our home.

Ultimately, demons (unclean spirits) were released, and it forced me to encounter, go to war with, and demolish for my sake and the sake of the bloodline and my family. My being subject to this type of hostile environment influenced certain behaviors, emotions, and thought patterns within me. It motivated some of the decisions that I had made in life.

Sin gives birth to sin, so parents must be careful about what type of spirits they allow to operate in their homes. You must understand that you are opening the door to and permitting influences to affect and possibly infect your children in the long run. Witnessing what my mother endured resulted in bitterness entering my heart.

This 'seed of bitterness' was the beginning of the enemy's plan to take control of my life. This kind of resentment opens the door to all kinds of perversions that seek to damage our spirits, our mental health, and our emotions. This was the entry that homosexuality crept through and invaded my life.

The Entry

Watching mom get beat by numerous male partners made me cold towards men. I lost romantic interest in the opposite sex based on what I watched my mother go through. Now understand this: just because I was disgusted with the idea of eventually entertaining a romantic relationship with a male counterpart, does not imply that I had romantic feelings for girls at that time either.

The enemy knew how to process me: lure and guide me into the position that he desired through various circumstances and encounters with certain people. He understood how to capitalize on the doors that I was persuaded to close through dysfunctional reasoning. Once the enemy interfered with my healthy relationship interests through calloused feelings and thoughts, he began to seduce me into exploring other types of relationship options: planting different ideas in my 14-year-old impressionable mind through other mislead peers.

Look! Did you catch that? That's it! Infiltrating thoughts is Satan's prime strategy to steal your mental, spiritual, and emotional freedom. He seeks to confuse and dilute the idea and the possibility of there being good men who can and will love, honor, and respect their woman. He entices you to embrace a spirit of bitterness that comes through lies and disappointment.

And with this sin struggle, that disappointment and hurt is usually because of a male figure. Maybe your dad abandoned you, or maybe your uncle sexually abused you, or perhaps your boyfriend cheated on you, and you contracted a sexually transmitted disease, or maybe your husband beat you. All these things can lead you from hurt to anger, to bitterness. If these things are left unaddressed, the latter will escort you down dark paths. And it all starts with an unrecognized and unaddressed trauma. It grows and branches into limbs of self-destruction and leaves of unforgiveness of self and others. Soon bitterness falls and becomes the death of you and the purpose and plan that God has for your life.

The enemy uses strategic methods, through our thoughts and those around us to lead us further away from the mind and heart of God. He introduces us to alternative options and lifestyles that should never be! Ephesians 4:31 says, "Get rid of all bitterness, rage, and anger, along with malice." It is the will and desire of God for our lives to be bitter free.

See, God knows how Satan uses bitterness and other emotions to rob you of your peace, freedom, and your true identity! Recovery from the effects of a shattered heart and this place of bitterness begins with forgiveness. As you learn to forgive and hold onto every Word of God, you'll start to transform into your new self! If you play your part, God will play and do His.

The Duty of Man and the Power of God

God has amazing plans for our lives, according to Jeremiah 29:11, and Satan has always hated us, and that plan. When you arrived on Earth, the enemy devised a scheme against you. Patiently he waits to work his strategy and launch an attack to snuff out your identity and purpose in God. He uses circumstances to try to wipe out your promise from God of being whole in spirit, soul, and body (1 Thessalonians 5:23).

He seeks to and knows how to infiltrate the family structure. He comes after this first. He uses a series of sinister tactics to lure us away and out of safety into a place of darkness through our pain and disappointment. He will come after those in authority first to weaken the structure or use their weaknesses to crack the foundation. Once we learn how to crack the code of deception and break the power of sin off our lives, we will be able to recover all and keep all for many generations to come!

The whole duty of man is to obey God and keep His commandments (Ecclesiastes 12:13). There is safety in doing what God says to do and how He says to do it. God intends to protect and provide for us: never to deprive us of *any* good thing. He's a loving Father who desires to restore us to our original created posture of dominion, being blessed and whole on every side, living in and with His peace, with every need met!

His restoration is successful when we turn, run back to, surrender to, obey, and trust Him. When we are obedient and live by His Word, He will make every crooked thing (including us) straight in our lives. I am a witness! When deception would have had me bound by the chains of homosexuality, a counterfeit relief to my pain, the Love of God proved to be much more satisfying!

My Heavenly Father has never left me or abandoned me! In all truth, I am no longer a forsaken orphan but adopted as the beloved of God. I am no longer drowning in my pain and sin but redeemed by the blood of the Lamb to tell the whole world of God's wondrous works and goodness! I once lived the lifestyle of a stud, but God rebuilt my shattered heart and made me "stunning" in His eyes

A Message to My Younger Me

Dear Younger Me,
It's not your fault, but it's your fight! I have called you a prophet to the nations. Trouble and suffering in this life are sure to come but be encouraged and shout with the voice of triumph for King Jesus has overcome this wicked world! Always remember this: at the end of the battle, the prize outweighs the pain! If you refuse to give up or give in, God has a reward waiting for you at the end of the race. Your treasure, in the end, will make it all worth it. God is fair. He will pay you according to what is due to you if you continue to persevere to the journey's end and refuse to faint! Some things may be blurry now, but it will all make sense in a little while. If you learn to forgive infinitely, love fearlessly, and endure indefinitely, nothing will be impossible for you. When you master these disciplines, there is no good thing

that the Lord will withhold from you! You will be sure to clear every hurdle and become more than a conqueror in every area of your life. If God is for you, the whole world can't stand against you! Honor your mother; this is the first commandment from the Lord that comes with a promise. Long life and success come with honoring your parents! Be humble, merciful, kind, and obedient no matter what you encounter. These traits are a great treasure in the sight of God. Regardless of what you may have lacked or lost, favor is on your life and you are destined for greatness beyond your wildest dreams. Love your mother despite every set back, and despite her faults and struggles, completely forgive her from your heart. Your healing and freedom depend on it! It is a true saying: The Lord will never leave you nor forsake you. Run with patience, run with joy...and see what the end will be!

Beautifully made in the Image of God,
Rachel

Angel Richardson

Angel is a wife and mother of three teenage children – a daughter and twin boys - and she is also mom to fur babies. She has a 30-year career in the technology industry, where she's held roles in Corporate Events, Channel Marketing, Client Services and Management, and Software Training & Implementation. Her mother instilled the love of serving others in her at a young age. She has imparted the same in her children. Angel and her family serve at their church and have also taken mission trips to Haiti and the Dominican Republic. When not working or serving, Angel enjoys cooking, hanging out with her family, tap dancing, and taking guitar lessons.

Fight To Be Free
~ *by Angel Richardson* ~

What does it mean to be free? For me, it means no longer being under the control of feelings and thoughts that I developed as a child – feelings that, from time to time, creep into my heart or mind and take me back to that place where I first experienced these thoughts or feelings. I wish these things could be outgrown, like clothes or shoes, but I haven't outgrown them yet. Sometimes, it's a daily struggle. I struggle with never being good enough or never having enough. Am I the only one?

Absolutely, not! I know many women (and men) who struggle with the same feelings of not measuring up in life. Sadly, social media doesn't help. People seem to post their "best lives" or "highlight reel" as I like to call it. They rarely post what they're truly going through and let's be honest…it's because most of us would rather see "feel good" posts vs. a post about someone's struggles. For those of us who struggle with never measuring up, social media can increase these feelings. We compare our own lives to what our friends are posting on social media and wonder how they can go on vacations, get new cars, or buy a new house when we're struggling to make ends meet. It's time to break free!

I honestly cannot remember the first time I realized that we were poor, but I do remember my mom struggling to make ends meet. I grew up in a single-parent household and am the oldest of four girls. There is an eight-year difference between my youngest sister and me. I was ten years old when my mom and dad officially separated, although my earliest memory of us not being together as a family was sooner than that.

My family moved from Chicago to Indiana when I was five years old. I only remember three houses where we lived together as a family; one was a trailer in a trailer park when we first moved back to Indiana. The other two were houses that were just one street over from each other. My parents never owned a home. We always rented from someone else. When I was younger, I didn't know the difference between renting and owning. All I knew was that it was our home.

Regardless of the status of my parent's relationship, my mom always made sure that we felt secure and that wherever we lived was our home. Her ability to do these things would be needed many times throughout my childhood.

Homeless

The only job I ever remember my dad having is in an ink factory. I don't think that he made a lot of money and, if he did, he was too busy going out with his friends or chasing women instead of providing for his family. Don't get me wrong I loved my dad. Looking back over my life, I can recall times when he could have done more to help my mom raise us girls. One example is when I was eight years old. My mom (who was pregnant with my youngest sister), my two sisters and I were homeless for about two weeks. We previously lived in a house as a family, but when my dad didn't pay the rent, we were evicted.

My dad said that he was going to stay with a friend, which we later found out was his girlfriend. My mom, sisters, and I spent a couple of days with my mom's friend Marlene. Mom and Marlene met each other at church and became close friends. Marlene, her husband, and two kids, graciously opened their tiny two-bedroom home to us. This living arrangement, however, soon proved to be quite stressful for everyone. Eight people in a home, made for two to four people at the most, was taking its toll on everyone.

Although mom was thankful for Marlene's generosity, she knew that we could not continue to stay with her and her family. The Pastor of our church heard about our situation and let us live in an apartment at the church, which they typically used for traveling evangelists who came into town for revivals. We stayed there until he was able to secure a place for us in a low-income public housing complex. The church paid the first month's rent, which was $26.00. God brought people into our lives to help us break free from homelessness. There were times when my mom struggled to pay the rent, but God always provided a way for us to pay our bills. We were never homeless again.

Making Something Out of Nothing

My mom was always amazing at making "something out of nothing" when it came to meals. She continues this ability even today. Sadly, and often, some of the foods that I ate as a kid are things that I don't eat very much as an adult. My mom took a job at a local head start school. Head Start is a free, federally funded program designed to get children between 3 and 5 years old ready for school. Not only did my mom work at the local head start, but a couple of my sisters attended the school.

Whenever the government delivered a shipment of butter and cheese to the school, the Director would set a box aside for us. She would always give us enough to last a month or so. The cheese, kindly referred to as "government cheese," came in a big three-pound block similar in shape and taste to a block of Velveeta cheese today. The butter was in a big one-pound block. Sometimes, our box would also include bags of rice.

I remember having A LOT of rice growing up. We would have it as a side dish with dinner or as hot cereal. To get us to eat the rice, my mom had to be creative. Putting butter and sugar on the rice made it more of a treat, in our minds, so we ate it. As a kid, I referred to this dish as "rice with butter and sugar." Pretty original, huh? In addition to rice with butter and sugar, my mom would use the butter and cheese to make grilled cheese sandwiches.

Also, the butter was delicious on popcorn. Some nights our dinner would consist of a grilled cheese sandwich and popcorn. We didn't have a microwave, so we cooked our popcorn on the stovetop. To this day, I still like popcorn cooked on top of the stove with lots of butter instead of the microwave kind.

Mom would also stock up on meat anytime it was on sale. When she cooked pork chops, she would remove the meat pieces off the bones when we finished eating. Later in the week, she would make gravy (which she made from flour, water, and seasonings), add the pork pieces, and serve it over rice. That would be our meal. There were many times that we didn't have milk for cereal. Mom had learned, when she was younger, that she could take canned milk, add water to it, and make the milk go farther.

We would use that milk for cereal or another meal that we called "toast, sugar and milk." It was toasted bread with butter, sugar, and milk on top. It probably does not sound good now, but when I was a kid, I loved it!! Some of my favorite meals included fried bologna or hot dogs with eggs for breakfast, salmon patties (made from canned salmon) and rice, beanie weenies (sliced hot dogs with pork and beans) with fried potatoes and onions, ham and beans, and Braunschweiger on crackers. If you're not familiar with Braunschweiger, it's a spreadable sausage made from pork liver. It doesn't sound appetizing, but it was so good! I still see it in stores today but have not purchased it since I was a kid.

Making Ends Meet

Our family took advantage of the food stamp program. It required households to purchase their stamps; for example, Mom could buy $200's worth of food stamps for $21.00. This small amount of food stamps had to provide enough food for the entire month. Food stamps, then, were paper and were in little booklets, according to denominations. For example, there were one-dollar stamps, five-dollar stamps, and ten-dollar books.

Today, all your allocated food stamps, called SNAP Benefits, are on a debit card. I remember getting embarrassed about using food stamps. What if my friends saw me? Would they know that my family didn't have any money? Would they tell other people that we were poor? Would they still want to be my friend? I can honestly say that I never lost a friend because my family had to use food stamps or live in government housing.

I'm not sure how the food stamp program works today, but when I was a child, you could only use them to purchase food items. To get money for the non-food household items we needed, such as toilet paper, laundry detergent and cleaning supplies, we would collect glass soda bottles and turn them in for cash – receiving two cents for each one. We also collected aluminum cans and turned those in for cash. From time to time, we would use food stamps to make a small purchase and use the change for household items. For example, buying five packets of Kool-Aid (orange and cherry were my favorites) for twenty-five cents and using a five-dollar stamp. We'd then use the $4.75 cash for cleaning supplies, or what have you.

Another way my mom made ends meet was by working. Once we were a little older, she began working outside the home. She almost always worked three jobs at one time to provide not just life's necessities but also things we wanted. She worked in an office during the day, and at night helped international college students with their English and other college courses. I've always said that she could have graduated from college multiple times due to the work she did with the international students. They paid her well for her help and even considered her their second mom.

Once the students graduated and went back to their home country, they would tell their siblings and friends to "look up Donna when you get to school, and she will help you." Having the students in our home multiple times a week not only provided income for our family but also opened a new world for us as we learned about their culture. I attribute so many things to my mom, one of them being my strong work ethic. She instilled this strong work ethic in my sisters and me, which has been evident throughout our lives.

Losing my Dad

After years of working with life coaches and some therapy, I traced much of my initial feelings of abandonment and not being "enough" from when my mom and dad separated. Why did my dad not want to stay? Was being a dad to us not good enough for him? Was I not good enough for him? Could we ever measure up to who he wanted or needed us to be? Unfortunately, these feelings carried over into other relationships in my life. Often, when I would get into a relationship with a guy, my mind would begin to focus on whether he was going to leave me just like my dad left me. It became hard to focus on the good in our relationship. I'd find myself wondering how long I'd be the focus of his attention before he started seeking someone else. These thoughts would only bring to light my insecurities, causing my relationships to end.

One day, just a few months shy of my 13th birthday, we received a call that my dad was in the hospital and had had a stroke. He was only 44 years old. He never recovered from the stroke and passed away, leaving my mom, sisters, and me for good. Because he and my mom had stayed close friends, his death was hard on all of us. What gave us comfort at this horrible time, however, was that dad accepted Christ on his deathbed, and we will reunite with him again in Heaven.

Although the feelings of "never enough" were triggered by my relationship with my dad, I am thankful for a mom who never made me feel this way growing up. My mom is an extraordinarily strong woman who did a great job raising my sisters and me. None of us would be the compassionate, hardworking, loving, family-oriented woman that we are today if it weren't for her. Her strong faith in God and His ability to see us through some tough times was something we relied on a lot! Faith and relationship with God are two things that I rely on each day.

Faithfulness

At a young age, my mom introduced us (me and my sisters) to God. We liked to joke that my mom had a real drug problem that we girls had to endure – she dragged us to church Sunday morning, Sunday night, Wednesday night, and any other night that the church was open. All kidding aside, she didn't have a real drug problem, but she did drag us to church a lot. Unlike most of today's churches, there were little distractions during service, so I learned a lot about God and his faithfulness. This began my love for God and my faith in Him.

Mom practiced faith a lot. The Bible tells us in Hebrews 11:1 that *"Faith shows the reality of what we hope for; it is the evidence of things we cannot see"* (New Living Translation). She had faith that God would provide for our family when every circumstance showed us that what she was hoping for couldn't happen.

One afternoon, we went to the grocery store to purchase something to make for dinner. We had some food stamps leftover and a little change. As we pulled into the parking lot and found a parking spot, we noticed a bag on the bottom of a shopping cart. We waited in our car for over fifteen minutes, thinking that someone would come back and claim their left behind groceries, but no one did. My mom looked inside the bag and found that the items we came to purchase were in the bag. Thank you, Jesus! We walked into the store and went to the office to see if anyone reported a bag of food missing.

She had faith that God would provide for our family when every circumstance showed us that what she was hoping for couldn't happen.

The lady at the office told us to keep it. We had a special treat that night as God had placed a large roast in our bag from Heaven. Growing up, one of my favorite songs was, "I've Never Seen the Righteous Forsaken" by Dallas Holm. In the song, he sings, "I've never seen God's people with a need that He could not meet. I know that He cares for His own, and His promises He'll keep." I learned that day, and many after it, that God cares about everything we care about…no matter how big or small.

A Christmas to Remember

Our first Christmas without my dad was one big miracle. We had no money, no food, and had a small tree that someone had discarded. We made our decorations from construction paper and salt and water (to hold the construction paper together). We also had picture ornaments. A teacher from school knew that many families couldn't afford school pictures, so she kept a small one from the packages (before sending them back) and had the kids make ornaments out of them.

We went to bed, after reading the Christmas story, from the Bible, looking forward to the next morning. Mom would later tell us that she had no idea where food or gifts were coming from, but she wasn't worried. A knock at the door was the beginning of our Christmas miracle. Mom's friend Marlene was a seamstress and had made all of us matching blouses. She had wrapped them and put them under the tree and handed mom $20 that a man from church had told her to give us.

Later, there was another knock at the door. This time, a teenager from the church was standing there with his father. They had two giant boxes containing gifts, a large turkey, and enough food for a month! The man had been fighting the VA for ten years, for disability pay, and received a check (with back pay) two days before Christmas. He wanted to give us a Christmas we would never forget, and he certainly did. We went to bed, not knowing where our meal or gifts would come from, and God used others to bless us that year.

Time with Mom

As I mentioned, my mom was a woman of strong faith. She was also busy raising four girls on her own. Regardless of what mom had going on in her day, she never let us get on the school bus without saying a quick prayer first, even if we missed the bus and had to walk. Before bed each night, we sat in a circle, on the floor, with dad's photo in the middle and had devotions and bedtime prayers. Prior to my dad's passing, one of our prayers was that he would accept Jesus into his heart. We knew that we wouldn't want to be in Heaven someday without him, and as I said earlier, that prayer was answered.

Each day after school, my mom would spend 15 minutes with us individually; she wanted to let us know how special we were to her. During our time together, we could tell her about our day and anything else we had on our hearts. To this day, the time I spend with mom is so special. We don't live in the same city, but I know that I can call her anytime I need her.

Sometimes, I just want to check on her. Sometimes, I want to tell her about something my kids have done or ask her to pray for me because I'm having a rough day. Other times, I wish I were that little girl having my 15 minutes of dedicated, uninterrupted, alone time with my mom. They were special memories that I'll always cherish.

Challenges of Growing up in a Small City

In addition to the challenges of living below the poverty level, being bi-racial was challenging as well. Bi-racial families were not as common back then as they are today. My sisters and I endured a lot of bullying. Not only were we in a lower economic class, we were not white. My mom was white, but my sisters and I were not. In middle school, I remember some of the black girls I was friends with telling me to pick a side. They wanted me to decide to be friends with the black kids or white kids but not both. I had friends of all races, and I wasn't about to choose sides. The girls realized that I wasn't going to choose one or the other and eventually let things go.

The challenge of being bi-racial followed me into adulthood when many parents of guys I dated wouldn't talk with me or want to spend time with me because I wasn't white. Once again, the feeling of not being good enough surfaced. "If only they would get to know me, they wouldn't care about my skin color" is a phrase I've repeated one too many times in my life.

Throughout my life, I've had friends of all social-economic backgrounds. In middle and high school, I had friends who were very wealthy and poor friends...like us. Of some of the wealthy friends – one had a small plane, and another girl had grandparents who owned a local department store. These girls had the latest fashions that my mom couldn't afford to buy me. I was thankful that my mom worked in an office at Indiana State University, and her boss had a daughter that was the same size as me. I would get her hand-me-downs, which were in excellent condition.

When she finished wearing her Calvin Klein jeans and Polo shirts, her dad would give them to my mom for me. I didn't care that they were hand-me-downs; I was just happy to be fashionable like the other kids.

Good Enough in a Not so Good Way

I was a shy kid growing up, which, I think, made me an easy target for abuse. My earliest memory of being abused was in the first grade. I was at recess and one of my male classmates pushed me up against the wall and put his hand in my crotch. I never told my parents about this incident, but after this happened; I would get sick every morning and be better as soon as the bus left. When mom pressed me about why I was acting sick, and what happened at school, I made up an excuse. I told her that a boy looked up my dress at lunchtime. While this certainly could have been true, I don't remember. My mom went to the school and talked with the teacher.

Because I was embarrassed about each situation, I never told anyone.

Things eventually got better at school, and I stopped getting sick every morning. Another time was around the 7th or 8th grade when my babysitter laid in my bed at bedtime and touched me inappropriately. The last time was when I was 15. This abuse is the one that emotionally affected me the most. I used to run errands with the Sunday school superintendent of my church. He was an older, married gentleman who always treated me like a daughter, except for *the* day.

One afternoon, we were out running errands and stopped by his house. I didn't think anything about it because we had visited on other occasions. However, on this particular day, he put me on the bed and began touching me inappropriately. I was in shock! We never had sex, but my relationship with him changed after that day.

Because I was embarrassed about each situation, I never told anyone, not even my mom. I suppressed the memories until I was in my 30's. I was watching an episode of Oprah, and she was sharing her story of abuse. Suddenly, memories of my abuse came flooding into my mind. I couldn't believe that I had forgotten about each incident, but that's what often happens.

To shut out the hurt, shame, and embarrassment, we tend to push ill thoughts and feelings far down into our memory – sometimes for years, until something or someone causes them to resurface. Looking back over my life, I can see how these three incidents of molestation affected me. I was a promiscuous teenager and young adult. I was good hanging out and having sex, but I knew that wasn't the way that I should be living my life. I wish I had the confidence to talk with my mom or someone else I trusted when the incident happened at 13. If I had, maybe at 15 I could have prevented another person thinking it was okay to use me for their perverted pleasure.

Sixteen

As with most teenagers, becoming 16 is a big deal. Sixteen was a time for firsts for me, one being I could finally date. My mom had strict rules when it came to dating. For example, the guy had to knock on the door to pick me up. He had to agree to have me home no later than my 11pm curfew. Sixteen was also the year that I graduated from high school. I graduated at 16 because I changed from the big high school to an alternative school when I was a sophomore. I used to have terrible menstrual cramps as a teenager, which would cause me to miss at least two days of school each month. Since I was absent so much, my mom decided to enroll me in an alternative high school. It was a smaller school, which allowed for individualized attention. I had teachers who took an interest in my education and seeing me succeed.

When I graduated high school, I had a two-year, full-ride scholarship to Vincennes University in southern Indiana. Sadly, I didn't take advantage of that opportunity. Instead, I stayed at home and worked so I could help my mom. I completed several college classes over the years but never obtained my college degree. The work ethic that my mom instilled in me as a kid has served me well into adulthood. I have worked hard in my career in the technology industry and have been successful.

When I was 18, my curfew changed from 11pm to 1am because I was dating a police officer who got off work late. If I hadn't been dating him, my curfew still would have been 11pm because as my mom always said, "Nothing good ever happens at midnight." I also had a job at McDonald's, so I could help my mom with rent and purchase some of the things I wanted. I received my driver's license and experienced the freedom that being a licensed driver brings.

I also got my first car, which my mom's friend helped me find. It was a blue 1964 Plymouth Valliant. It had a bench seat in the front and push buttons on the dashboard that would be my gears. The car, although older than me, was pretty cool.

God's Faithfulness

My life has been full of ups and downs – the good and the bad. I am, however, reminded of Romans 8:28. It says, *"And we know that God causes everything to work together for the good of those who love God and are called according to his purpose for them"* (New Living Translation). As horrible as it was to think that God would use our poverty, my dad abandoning his family, my dad's death, or my molestation for good, that's what happened.

By experiencing each of these things in my life, I can be there as an encouragement for others. I can empathize with what they're going through and offer hope that only God can give. With God's help, we can all break free of the circumstances and mistakes of the past and become all that God intended us to be.

A Message to My Younger Me

Dear Younger Me,

*Oh, sweet girl, there are so many things that I want to tell you. Right now, you feel as though you don't measure up, that you're not good enough for anyone or anything. You want to be accepted by everyone you meet and will seek acceptance in ways that aren't always good. I am here to tell you that YOU ARE ENOUGH! You are accepted and loved by your family and God. Dad will leave and find another woman to love. Please know that this doesn't mean that he doesn't love Mom or you and your sisters. He is struggling with his feelings of acceptance and keeps searching for it in others. You did nothing wrong! People will hurt you but **be strong**! Rely on that feeling in your gut to guide you. Find someone that you trust to process how you're feeling. Do not be ashamed of what happens to you. You did nothing* *wrong! Learn to forgive those who hurt you. Forgiveness is hard, especially when you feel wronged or hurt by someone; however, forgiveness isn't for the other person, it's for your own healing. I've heard it said, "forgiveness doesn't make them right; it makes you free." Your success in life will be based upon your determination and hard work. You will accomplish great things! Have a relationship with God. Talk with Him, in prayer, every day. He will guide your life and show up in ways that you can't even imagine. Lastly, love yourself. Serve others. Be a loyal friend. Be kind. Know that you are beautiful, smart, confident, a hard worker, strong, generous, creative, grateful, valuable, worthy, more than enough, and FREE!*

Beautifully made in the Image of God,
Angel

Lauren Nowlin

Lauren, a native Hoosier. Through self-awareness, she learned to love herself. This self-love came from her passion for HUGS! Lauren advocates for self-love through an initiative of Healing, Understanding, and Growth. Reared in a Christian household, Lauren was curious about how people work together in their community. Her upbringing, coupled with her collegiate studies of Spanish Language and Culture at IUPUI, further developed her innate love for youth and community. Cultivating that love extensively through the Edna Martin Christian Center, Lauren gained the perspective of servant leadership and wholeheartedly believes in altruism in everyday life. She is the founder of The Nowlin Group and she has served as an advisory board member for The Felege Hiywot Center, GRoE Inc., and The M.A.C. Center, Inc.

Son Shine
~*by Lauren Nowlin* ~

When the Sun Shines too Bright

"You turned my wailin' into dancin'. You turned my sorrow into joy. You make my heart sing, can't keep silent. I'll sing praises forever more." The words to Donald Lawrence & Company's song blasted as I pranced around the room. I sang at the top of my lungs while choreographing movement I imagined 'wailin' and 'dancin' would look like while the track repeated the calypso type beat against the soft blue painted walls of my room. I danced and moved and sang my heart out as the sun shined through my window, warming each step I took.

I have always wanted to dance. Not just any dance; I wanted to do ballet, which required technique merged with talent that I treasured. Never mind my awkward expression of music or unoriginal movement to melodies. I wanted to be a statuesque articulation of musicality. Typically, a ballerina is a tall swan, moving gracefully from position to pose with poise and posture. At a young age, I believed I could be a ballerina because I was tall. Grown women appeared much taller in the mirror of my childhood imagination than real life. But when mom enrolled my sister and me in ballet and tap and jazz, respectively, at Stars Dance Studio, it allowed me to flaunt my newfound height.

My growth spurt came before everyone else around me at the time. I blossomed early like a precious tulip before her time. I was what you would call an "early bloomer." As many melanated girls often do, I physically matured early. Simultaneously, my mental maturation developed discernment for others' needs that made me appear quite noetic.

Even as a child, I was an empath, I sympathized with the sun. The warmth of its touch and embrace upon my cacao colored skin made me feel lit on the top of a hill. The rise and set of the sun fueled me with energy as I moved to stretch and sway as I grew. Born in the summer, I was a sun baby and could not get enough of it. I longed for it; I embraced the season and its temperatures more than any other. I loved to run around barefoot, with the sun beaming down on me like boiling beams of light. When I felt the "Sonlight" on me, it was the Source giving me energy and saying it is time to grow.

Until about twelve years old, I towered over everyone. This age is the same age when Christ began to teach in the synagogue. Suddenly, I stopped growing vertically. I seemed to shrink from adults' line of vision as my peers began to blossom and develop around me. No longer was I alone at the top of the hill. I hid in the shadow of other people's expectations. I had gone from being the one leading the charge, often with my friends and siblings, to the last in line, literally by height. I became passed over by my peers for things like hanging out after school or being the girl to date. The shorter I felt, the more outspoken I became. My siblings would say I was a know-it-all, bossy even. From a young age, I had a way of telling people what to do in a positive way that encouraged them while also being extremely assertive. What happens when you bloom first? What spotlight is on you? What wanted, and unwanted, attention do you draw when the sun and the Son shine bright on you?

I came across as "all grown up;" acting or trying to be "grown" was what adults called it. Though this was how I was perceived, it was not how I felt. I was not yet aware of how tall my spirit appeared. And, as a result, I came to believe that no one thought to nurture the sprout that blooms first. They lent their focus to those that blossomed later, which seems to be when they are ready to pay attention, or they deem it is time to take care of it. The gardener tends to the ones still budding and pays special attention to the late bloomers. Often, and unfortunately, by then, the early bloomer has either dried up or been choked out by weeds or attached to wildflowers that can grow up with the most beautiful flower. Little did I know my sprout would become not a blossom, but a burning bush attracting moths to my sun fueled flames!

The gardener tends to the ones still budding and pays special attention to the late bloomers.

Fatal Attraction

"We attract what we lack." Words of wisdom Dr. Tuesday Tate spoke as I shared reflecting on people that had come in and out of my life. If that was the case – if we attract what we lack – my formative years must have been void of emotion, because the drama that surrounded me was more than a little bit from the opposite sex. Dr. Tate continued to explain that men are often attracted to the anointing or gifts you have on your life, and some may come to try and control or destroy it. Every person that comes in your life is there for a specific reason.

There is always an exchange that takes place. Each relationship you will ever have has a commencement and a destination: and the vehicle, in which it travels, is fueled by perspective and emotion. Kinships and mentorships often found me in the passenger seat awaiting a destination: sightseeing on the road while enjoying the incredible playlists of others' experiences from their lips to my ears, I began to be fueled by the energy of people - people at school, in the sanctuary, and at service projects - as they shared what was visibly a passion of theirs.

Anyone who had been anywhere else and was willing to share about it intrigued me. I thought I did not have a story to tell or anything anyone would want to listen to, but I hunted for others' life experiences, especially ones different than my upbringing. That is how I learned to enjoy stories.

So, then I met this guy; he was a great storyteller. I mean, when I first saw him, I was drawn to him like something from a movie. In hindsight, a cloud of smoke billowed around him; I should have heeded it as a warning. Through my impressionable eyes, it appeared the whole room disappeared except for him. I thought that something, that gravitational pull that kept me running back into him for the next eleven years of my life, was love. For a time, it was companionship.

Today, I recognize it as familiarity. We were attracted to each other's analogous love of music and nerd acumen. I was in love with his love of things: things that were not familiar. I celebrated and highlighted his relationship with hip-hop, his beautiful works of prose. And most of all, his ability to speak his mind fearlessly. He was a black man who knew the Word of God, the plight of a Black man and the banter of a thespian. I esteemed what he could do higher than what I could not bring myself to express.

But what did I love about me? What could I celebrate for myself? Why did my scholarly accomplishments and religious dedication pale in comparison to his life lived in full? There was an unknown world that he had experienced, and I wanted it vicariously. When I met him, I was a junior in high school. He was in a relationship with someone else.

Eleven years later, when our 'situationship' – a friend with benefits equivalent to a complicated, undefined, label-less relationship - finally came to an end; I found myself back where I started; alone and purposeless.

Finding meaning in other people devalues the purpose of you. The journey of self-discovery starts with understanding that there are some things that must be done alone. "To thine own self be true" but first find out who thine own self wants, and is really meant, to be. Travel the road that leads you to love you, first. Then, anywhere you go will have a history of self-love to guide your way and fuel your next interpersonal excursion. At the end of this trip, I learned, most of all, how I wanted to be loved.

Some relationships are road trips, adventures on the cusp of the next exchange of energy you have with another person. They are incredible, once in a lifetime experiences with deep emotions and memories that you will fondly reminisce and retell whenever the thought of that person crosses your mind. My childhood friendships are these types of trips. They give me life every time I think about a late-night rehearsal for a youth church program or breakfast at Papa's diner before a high school state orchestra competition.

Other relationships are like staycations that interrupt your daily routine but are not far from your regularly scheduled program. Girls nights with takeout and a Grey's Anatomy marathon, or video chatting with cousins in other states, was enough to make me feel like I was on vacation. Still others can be like a daily commute that holds its value hidden in plain sight; for example, talking to your siblings while living at home or Monday morning chats with your coworkers when you come back to work from the weekend.

These trips are easy to take for granted and not appreciated until absent. Unlike a staycation, which is often for rest and refocusing, these kinds of trips are more consistent and therefore gain higher mileage whenever you reach your destination and commence a new journey.

I draw your attention to these examples to encourage you. Please be mindful of the types of 'ships' that travel in and out of your life. One ship I was seeking in others was a mothership. I had started listening to bros over the voice of the pros in my life. Later in life, my mom would tell me that I should always trust the ones who know me best.

Growing up and being "voluntold" to participate in things created this feeling of necessity in me. I knew that there were causes everywhere, and when I learned of a new one, I immediately donned my invisible cape of care and action. Later on, life taught me that heroes are not to wear capes of any kind.

NO CAPES! So, instead of flying, I would live my life thinking I needed to be on a particular ship. All along, God was preparing me to stretch beyond the horizon.

Stunted Growth

I am a child at heart. I always have been. I never wanted to grow up. My Walt Disney level of optimism fueled that sentiment. Growing up on movies, television, and soundtracks, I animated a portrait of the world that made me feel like anything was possible. At my official height of four feet eleven and a half inches, I was too tall to qualify as a little person and shorter than the average bear.

In my preteen years, I shot up a head above most everyone else! My two brothers and sister, my cousins at church, and my friends at school. Fast forward to my junior year of college, and according to The Walt Disney Company, I now qualified as cast member in the 'happiest place on earth'! We, my sister, and I, were accepted in the Disney College Program, and I landed a role in the cast of a show called *The Studio Backlot Tour*.

I narrated a ride through old sets and movie props, past the Catastrophe Canyon, and through a costume shop where clothes, from some of the movies I grew up watching, were displayed in their childhood-imaginative glory. After stalking a movie starring a princess that looked like me who fell in love with an amphibian, worked hard, invested her wages, and became an entrepreneurial restaurateur. From this tale, "The Princess and The Frog," I realized I had not yet achieved adulthood. I had plans I wanted to accomplish and had not yet, but I was almost there.

A consistent question asked of me, growing up, was, "What do I want to do and be when I was older?" My dad worked as a mechanical engineer. He created solutions to vehicular situations daily. He told me to be true to myself and don't try to be anyone else. Live in my strengths; don't focus on my weaknesses. Incredible wisdom from an incredible man but way easier said than done. My mom was an educator. She taught students in public schools for years until she became an administrator and retired.

Career choices from my parents leaned towards the fields of law and medicine. I vacillated between anesthesiology, immigration law, and everything in between. Yet, one day, I exclaimed to my mom, "I want to be a teacher when I grow up!" Her response, "No, you don't!" It was clear; teaching was absolutely out of the question. At least that is what my mom said. My parents wanted me to be better than them. So, I settled on becoming the first female president of the United States of America. At least that was my plan. God planned on showing me that this plan was NOT His. After being admitted to a handful of colleges, I settled on the alma mater of my older brother as they offered the most scholarship money. I studied hard but always wondered what it would have been like to attend an HBCU like my parents.

Going to a predominantly commuter college, I would get dropped off on one end and would be at the opposite end by time classes was over. I was studious, and all that walking to class four days a week kept me from the infamous freshman fifteen! Strategically, I enrolled in political science, Spanish, and culture courses to become the immigration lawyer I had professed and desired to become. I targeted my plan. It would get me to law school, then to the Senate in time to gain ground for my presidential run as the first African American female of the United States.

Then, God demonstrated just how much my plan meant to Him. Remember when I said time was a gift? It truly was. I had spent my college years in and out of my parents' house and student housing. I was growing further and further from the religion of ritual movement and rote memories of how things used to be before my older brother moved to California. I missed my brother, but I was glad to be out of his line of vision that echoed my mother's sentiments of extracurricular activity: going to church and staying away from the opposite sex.

My focus shifted from family to festivity and the guys I had attracted were the perfect fix. All the Son Shine I was so used to receiving paled in the fluorescent light of fleeting links to the one thing I was advised to stay away from while growing up, the pollinators formally known as boys.

Have you ever stared into space and forgot where you are? I remember the many times in grade school when my attention navigated toward the emptiness of the earth called space. My focus was on the outside, wondering what life was all about. My dad always used to say, "There is a knowing in your eyes." To this day, I cannot tell you what he saw, but everywhere I looked, I saw things. I looked to those around me to tell me who I was and why I lived. Searching for my purpose was a steady pastime for me. I searched for it every day and finally discovered it when I stopped trying to fulfill everyone else's; when I found that I had no problem saying no.

Growing up, I participated in many things: community service activities to church services; afterschool events to recreational sports. On Saturday mornings, my siblings and I were at workshops, seminars, and other training. Oh my, how I wished I could have slept longer. I enjoyed all the people I met and gained so much insight and knowledge, I firmly believe that I would not be where I am today had I not been volunteered for all of those things. What rubbed off on me the most was the action and purpose of giving. Regardless of the cause, being needed became my call to action. When there was a need, I assumed it meant I was to fulfill it. Somewhere I had personally taken on the idea that every solution had to be fulfilled by me.

My first position after college was as a mentor. I was coordinating a youth after school and summer program for a community center. I tried to meet the needs that I saw and tried to be everything to everyone with a very candid conversation. My boss made a statement to me, about me, that was very hard to hear, "Lauren, I don't always tell you everything because you get over-involved." Over involved? Since when is seeing a need and doing what I can to meet it by any means necessary a bad thing? Oh, I get it; I see; I was doing too much! What I had not learned was that the ability to recognize where the needs are and then seeking out solutions was a gift.

FOMO: the fear of missing out. This fear is a new phobia that has plagued our culture to the point of addiction to social media notifications. The likes, views, shares, and comments are the obsessions of this era. My phobia was not missing out: it was what happens when I am not in a place to assist. I was obsessed with helping others. Why? Because my family built a culture of helping; it is an innate part of who I am. Nothing can better solidify understanding than the manifestation of the works that faith builds. But what happens when you have built up others and their faith, to the point that you have nothing left to give?

When obedience to requests is the cause of your self-sacrifice? Subconsciously, the words of 1 Corinthians 9:22-23 became my motto. My inner atmosphere, environment, and mindset were of urgency, and being all things to all people was the solution. My problem was this, I thought to fulfill the need and to be needed was love. So, when I began to stretch myself thin, trying to help everyone else, wisdom taught me how to say no.

NO!

I have an affinity to the administrative aspects of life called, by many, The Gift of Helps. My ideal job would be traveling around the world, giving hugs, working for food, and helping in whatever way I can. But in my twenties, the desire to help led me to fill my free time with other people fueling this insatiable need to be needed. By the time I got to a place of worship and a profession I had chosen on my own, I saw so many things that I was able to do. But I ignored all expediences and volunteered for everything. Wherever I was, I did not want to miss out on what God was doing.

So, in the ministries I attended, I inserted myself into every AMAZING thing God had given me the ability to see as a need. I was used to being in church every day of the week. I did not have extracurricular activities, so my appointment diary was inundated with other itineraries when my first ministry should have been to myself. I ran myself ragged volunteering for the causes of others because, as I learned from storytellers, other people's passion fueled me.

I was estranged from my family and gained passage through the gateway of volunteering with my spiritual and financial resources to others, particularly men that needed emotional understanding and developmental support, nearly abandoning my desire to command the most powerful country in the world. The strong, empowering, maternal influence my mother had on me translated to sympathetic and enabling. It drew men to me who had not grown up.

Two of them came at pivotal times when I, like a flower, began to develop in the areas God created and purposed me to display through my petals or gifts. A fog rolled in my mental state, what I recall now as 'the dark years,' and relationships without the distinction between boyfriend and a friend who is a boy, rolled into port more often than not.

The second of these two can be described as being attracted to my destiny, but it was here for my demise. I had to learn the difference between how to discern who was best for me. It took a while to understand it, but not knowing could have been fatal. The first situationship I formed was in my mind, and fashioned it into a courtship. Long talks on the phone and endless hangouts that would not be labeled as dates; I defined as something more. Why? Because, I was 'the friend' advising him on his chosen partnerships and ventures of romance and intimacy with women who were not me. I chased this ship on and off for eleven years until the other ship abruptly cut him off: claiming me as his, much like Columbus claimed to have discovered India.

The second vessel was a turbulent dictatorship that knocked me completely off course. Why was it when a man came dancing into my life, quoting scripture, and dripping in manipulation, was I willing to love him in exchange for the attention I felt I needed? Not only did I accept him as significant, but I asked him to move in and, as a result, stayed away from my family altogether. He was not the type of man you bring home to your family so, embarrassed, I took their rejection of him as a rejection of myself. I put my life, my plans, on hold while cheering on a man who did not want to move forward.

By the time I started to come to myself, he had drained me of all the Sonshine I had. I was emotionally isolated, told not to speak unless we were discussing scripture. The few times I went to see friends or coworkers, I was called names and demeaned for speaking my mind. I withdrew from the blossom of joy that I had bloomed into so many years ago. I had no idea how to get out of that relationship. I remember waking up one morning and thinking, '*God, how did my life come to this?'*

Not long after one of our bible studies, at home, he had left his cell phone on the kitchen table. Until the opportunity presents itself, you never think you will be one of those women who go through a person's cell phone. I took advantage of it: not for fear of missing out or expecting wrong, but mostly out of curiosity. God had begun to siphon the fog away, I believe, through the prayers of the family and friends who loved me and wanted me to come back home. I looked at his text messages and discovered two weeks' worth of relationship building, intimacy, and familiarity with a woman who was not me. Immediately the residue of fog was lifted.

Ultimately, I prayed the most earnest prayer to God. I prayed that He would help me release my desire for this man and any other, past, present, or future who is not supposed to be in my life. I prayed and allowed God to show me who He intended for me. In short, eleven years from my original plan, I told God that no matter what the outcome and who He had for me in the future, I would not continue to hold on to anyone if he was not the man for me. I just wanted, no I needed, to be done. I wanted to be free! I wanted to be happy! I had spent more than enough of my time, energy, and passion on someone who is not prepared to move forward with me in life.

Time is a precious gift that God gives you. Make time for you to get to know yourself. I focused on one person's love, affection, and scraps of time when I could have been getting to know myself. I was the same girl going into that space as I was coming out, because the relationship I was in did not augment me. Or so I thought. I had driven around in circles only to exit, very unromantically, in the same place I started: a girl looking for love. You may not see your growth until you look back on your journey. Your petals and leaves may not develop the way you thought they would. For sure, mine did not. Came nowhere close! But I was not stunted in my growth.

In fact, my darkest days were when I grew the most, stretching towards the beams of light that tended to shine when I needed them the most. Some places in my life matured while I focused on the most immature. Saying "I'm fine" when you are not is lying to yourself. People ask because they sincerely want to know. I have given more of myself to people not deserving than I care to remember. But one thing I never allowed people to do was to take the opportunity to help me heal by hearing how I was doing.

Do not reduce your sentiments and experiences to 'fine.' When you are happy, say so!

Do not reduce your sentiments and experiences to 'fine.' When you are happy, say so! When you are sad, say that too! Express how you feel and examine why you have come to feel that way. Then decide based on what is best for you and not based on how you feel. When you feel like the clouds are hovering over you, allow the rain; they come to water you and pour in all the energy you have given. When all other responses to your emotions shed no light on the clarity that comes with deciding, remember this word, "No." It is a complete sentence.

By saying yes to everyone, you are teaching yourself, and them, how to devalue you, not treasure you, or not love you. You need to set boundaries to recharge. Everything you see is not for you to solve. Be a master at what you are called to do, and don't try to be a jack-in-the-box: jumping at everything simply because you can do it. It may not benefit you. I am done wasting my time and concede to allowing the Son to shine on the things I am good at, which makes me shine just as bright.

A Message to My Younger Me

Dear Younger Me,

You are so beautiful. I am proud of who you are and everything you have endured to get to where you are today. I could not have planned the life you will live, but I definitely would live it again if I had to. You are going to go through some things. Times that are tough and tranquil and triumphant will all train you for the woman you are to be. Do not be scared. And please remember to enjoy every moment of being you. Things are not always going to turn out the way you expect, and that is ok. You can only react to the things you understand. Grow by learning new things instead of limiting yourself to the people and places around you. When you get the urge to write, do it. That is your spirit, preparing you for great things ahead. You and I both know you enough to tell you this with extreme confidence. "No" is a complete sentence. You are allowed and entitled to say no! Everything asked of you should always be answered honestly. If you do not want to do something, before you answer, ask yourself why you are doing it. And "because they asked" is not a legitimate answer. When you do not feel well, when you are having a bad day, hug yourself. Take time to heal, understand, and grow from those feelings BY YOURSELF. Lauren, you do not have to be ok all of the time. It is ok to be NOT FINE! Just know that your feelings are not facts; they are a reaction to your current situation. Analyze what has made you feel the way you do. Acknowledge the feelings that you are experiencing. Act after you understand what the best thing is to do, whether you feel like it is or not. And own every decision you make. It will all work out for your good. A final piece of advice I have for you is this: love yourself fearlessly the way you love others. Do not sacrifice yourself to love others the way you want love, in return. If you never receive advice on how to do that, I invite you to read 1 Corinthians 13, specifically verse 13. "But for right now, until that completeness, we have three things to do to lead us *toward that consummation: Trust steadily in God, hope unswervingly, and love extravagantly. And the best of the three is love." You are living the story of how I learned to love me. In loving myself, I learned the dance of life is a beautiful syncopation of not just who you are, but what you do. The type of dance is your choice, and the decisions you make put you under your stage spotlight every day. Son shine. I never became the ballerina I thought I would be. I was not tall enough to fulfill someone else's dance, but there was and is beauty through the dance of my life. Misty Copeland said, "the beauty of dance is being a part of something that is all you, from creation to performance." This number is all you.*

Beautifully made in the Image of God,
Lauren

Lisa Bellamy

Lisa resides with her husband, two sons, and Bella, their boxer (dog), in Indianapolis. She is the entrepreneurial leader of her own clinical social work business specializing in uplifting women and reunifying families. She has a health and wellness business and coaching practice, Midlife Makeover Lounge, where women can find their true purpose in life. Her goal? To help all women live in their greatness with vibrant health and mental fortitude. Ms. Bellamy is uniquely qualified from her work with families. She offers a no-nonsense approach to helping families reconcile and become mentally strong. Lisa's soulful mission is to help every woman leave a legacy that will outlive them and their children and to be a positive contributors to our world.

Worthy Is as Worthy Does
~by Lisa Bellamy~

Imagine you are enjoying the moment. You are happy and engaged in the activity that is taking place. Scrolling through social media, you see lots of people making posts, showing their cute outfits, their puckered lip selfies, their hair on fleek, and their "perfect" bodies. You are hitting the like button or tapping to like photo after photo.

So you think, "I can do that and I'm cute too." You want to make a post while you are wearing a new outfit that you purchased a few days ago. Your self-confidence is off the charts – HIGH! Using your phone's self-timer, you strike several different poses to take many photos. A friend takes some. While you are feeling yourself, you choose the one photo you like best.

You choose the best photo to post because you know you are looking hot. You write your caption, "I'm gorgeous" and hit the post button. You start seeing the likes and the love hearts flowing in and BAM! Someone makes a mal-intent statement about your appearance. You begin to see comments like: "You aren't pretty; girl, who told you that you are cute; you're fat; those clothes are ugly; you should just kill yourself because no one wants to see you." Because the negative comments continue, you decide to delete the post.

Just like that, your "I'm gorgeous" self-image dissipates. You start to focus on your flaws, and thoughts of being unworthy damage your self-belief. Inwardly, you believe those statements are true: outwardly, your behavior supports your belief. You start to hide how you feel, fighting against self-criticism, people-pleasers, and becoming vulnerable.

You know, the vulnerability can be extremely uncomfortable. Vulnerability is like when your naked body is about to be exposed in a room full of women with judgy eyes. The towel drops off your body exposing every insecurity you do not want anyone else to see. It is that feeling you resist when you are feeling pain or sadness.

At bedtime, you replay those negative comments rationalizing them with: "I don't care what they think. I am going to repost it because I do not care!" Then, the next day you go to school or work acting like everything is okay. However, you cannot escape the thoughts that maybe I'm not that cute; I should not have posted the photo. On and on and on, these negative thoughts invade your mind.

There are hidden roots to your feelings of unworthiness. It likely began long before your social media post that turned into a "neg-fest." It likely began by a well-intended adult in your childhood, or a bully, or a teacher, or a parent.

How does the negativity manifest when it originates from those who are supposed to protect and love you? Maybe it is internalized as self-hatred or unworthiness or people pleasing or self-criticism. Where did your path of unworthiness begin?

NOTE: *From this point forward, you will see the word "**LOADING**." Loading is to alert you that a feeling or belief is being inputted into your computer – your brain and self-image.*

Think back to **that** one time in your life before the posting of your Insta-selfie photo where you felt unworthy, unloved, or **just** different because you knew that person did not mean you well. What did that person say? How did it make you feel? Who was it? Where were you? I want to take this opportunity to demonstrate how to look back and identify that moment that took the wind out of your sail. While this was not the only incident from my childhood, this is the one that I believe incited feelings of unworthiness.

In the late '70s, I used to watch Jiminy Cricket, a cartoon about a talking cricket. Now, let me be clear. I was not a cartoon lover. I only liked three cartoons, Casper the

Friendly Ghost, Scooby-Doo and Jiminy Cricket. I believed them to be "happy" cartoons. They were the perfect opportunity for me to escape what was going on around me. Watching these cartoons was my way of numbing myself like social media is for others.

The Cricket was always uplifting and an escape from the dysfunction in my home. My home was one of those places that validated my feelings of unworthiness. One day, I was watching the Jiminy Cricket show and became very aware of the size of my forehead when an adult said, "You have a big forehead, just like Jiminy Cricket!" I remember their laugh that ensued. It was maniacal and went on for what seemed like hours

Vulnerability is like when your naked body is about to be exposed in a room full of women with judgy eyes.

(because I kept replaying that statement in my forehead [pun intended]). I looked in mirror after mirror hoping it was not true. It seemed like a bad thing to have a protruding forehead. After all, a protruding forehead makes you ugly - RIGHT?

LOADING...

UNWORTHINESS

"Your crown has been bought and paid for. All you have to do is put it on your head." ~James A. Baldwin

A quick search on Google defined *unworthiness* as *not deserving effort, attention, or respect.*

From that day forward, I always made sure that my hair was covering my forehead. I became extremely self-conscious of my appearance. I hid that feeling in my smile. I hid it in saying yes when no was more appropriate and complete. I hid it when I stayed in relationships that were not serving me. I hid it when I wanted to practice self-care. But back to unworthiness, which manifested in me as self-sabotaging all things great intended for me. It came from a person who was supposed to love me.

How did unworthiness "load" in my childhood computer (brain)?

So how did unworthiness manifest in my life? Unworthiness showed up as not feeling loved, and this resulted in erratic behaviors that began in kindergarten. While at the age of 4, I did not know it as seeking love it was. My kindergarten teacher had a disability that required her to use a scooter. I used to have tantrums, and the teacher would try to get me out of the room on her scooter. Most days, I would go in the hallway when requested.

However, there was one particular day that my tantrum was more intense than usual. I did not want to complete the task that was given to me; perhaps, I was feeling the need to be loved. I had ALL the teacher's attention. I knew the teacher could not get me out of the room while flailing my arms and legs. I was not going in that hallway! This self-seeking behavior for attention and love continued through third grade. In my mind, I knew if I did not want to look like a failure in front of everyone, looking like a "crazy child" would be better. It was the perfect way to get lots of attention.

In my perspective, the only way to feel worthy was to receive love from this person in my home. I would try to be the perfect child by washing the dishes, doing my homework without being asked, and going to bed without being told. I would try to do everything right to get love, but it never came in the way I thought it should. Since I felt it never appeared, I sought for it in other ways.

The strong desire to be loved invaded my friendships. I never thought that I was worthy of having friends. So, most of the time, I secluded myself and hid my feelings with a smile. Even though I didn't want anyone else to know that I felt unloved and unworthy of love, it became evident by the male friends that I chose. I stayed in those relationships longer than I should have while trying to help them to understand that they needed my love. In actuality, I was trying to fill the void of worthiness. It never came. It never arrived.

This thought of unworthiness still haunts me in different aspects of my life: not all aspects of my life, just some.

PAUSE

Journal Time: Think of an event that occurred in your life and made you feel unworthy. Are you still carrying that feeling with you (i.e., bad relationships, looking for worthiness in the wrong manner, or always seeking perfection, etc.)? Write this in your journal; journaling increases self-awareness (more on that later). When you feel unworthy, you make horrible relationship choices. You may hang out with the wrong people, or your significant other may not treat you fairly. You desire everything to be perfect because you do not want to be judged.

LOADING...
PEOPLE PLEASING

"Care about what other people think and you will always be their prisoner." ~Lao Tzu

The online Merriam-Webster dictionary defines people-pleasing as *a person who has an emotional need to please others often at the expense of his or her own needs or desires.*

Bingo! This is a perfect definition! Sometimes we people-please to the point that we disregard our values to make someone else happy; despite our need to feel the way we want. There was another time that I wanted my family to be proud of me. I was probably 12 years old and was in elementary school. I came home and noticed that there was a chicken thawing out in the kitchen sink. So, I completed my homework and my chores - dishes and vacuuming. By this time, the chicken had thawed.

I thought I would help by cooking dinner. It was one less thing my parents would have to do when they arrived home from work. I was so happy, frying that chicken. It was golden brown and looked perfect. However, it was quickly brought to my attention that I had wasted a "good chicken." To my dismay, it was still bloody on the inside. I felt horrible for wasting the chicken and for not making them happy.

This desire for people-pleasing showed up in way too many ways of my life. Like when I did not want my friends to be mad at me for not agreeing with their opinions of others or their beliefs. I would put my beliefs and opinions on hold to satisfy the friend. I would do this in relationships as well. I had a strong appearance of an outer shell and played a tough role, but inside I was dying trying to make sure that no one else's feelings were hurt.

The desires of my heart did not match my actions. Deep down, I mean way deep down, I just knew I was worthy of love. Whether I agreed with my friends or not or if I did all things right, I knew I was worthy. Because of those embedded strong beliefs of unworthiness and people pleasing, my mind misguided me.

PAUSE

I want you to create a trigger (a door closing, sirens, goosebumps, tightness in your body, a lump in your chest, etc.), which is your warning that you are about to people-please. Once your awareness is alerted: people pleasing LOADING...

I want you to create a mantra that will stop people pleasing in its tracks! Creating a mantra will increase self-awareness when you are about to put someone else's values before yours and you are about to devalue your self-love.

Here are a Few Mantras to consider:

I am enough.

I have a lot of worth to offer.

I am doing my best.

LOADING...
OVERLY SELF-CRITICAL

"You have been criticizing yourself for years, and it hasn't worked. Try approving yourself and see what happens." ~ Louise L. Hay

Here again, is another definition from Merriam-Webster's online dictionary. Self-Critical is defined as *inclined to find fault with oneself: critical of oneself.*

Since I felt that I was judged by others, albeit, teachers, parents, friends, boyfriends, etc., I internalized it and made that judgment my own. I felt that I deserved to be judged, so I should do it before others do it. I always felt that I was not good enough. In the 5th or 6th grade, we had these races during field day. I loved the car tire roll relay and was proud to participate.

The object of the race was to make the tire roll by slapping it with your hand across the finish line before your opponent did. I wanted to win so badly! I had demonstrated in practice that I was good at this game! But while preparing for the race, I heard an adult say that another student was better than me. I was deflated (pun intended). When I got on the track, I thought to myself, why even try?

Already thinking that I sucked, I did not give 100% effort. I gave it about 80% effort, and the person that they said would win, won! I was pissed! Do you hear me? PISSED! I was mad at the adult and blamed them for making me lose. Perhaps I could have won, but I will never know since I did not put forth the effort to win.

Another event occurred in my 11th-grade English class. I wrote what I thought to be the best English paper ever. However, my teacher thought otherwise. My pride was crushed when I saw my grade. As the teacher was explaining why I got a C+, she criticized my writing with laughter. I felt like she was demoralizing me. I could not believe that she, who was here to teach me, was laughing at me. This moment defined how I viewed my writing skills. From that point on, I was not comfortable sharing my thoughts in writing.

Even through college, when I had to write a paper, I could hear her laugh. EVERY...SINGLE...TIME! Eventually, I started to procrastinate to prevent myself from revisiting this experience. Oh, and by the way, this event repeated itself while I was working on my masters. Albeit, I had more fight within me this time. I made sure the professor knew, in an utmost respectful way with a dose of assertiveness, that her behavior was unacceptable.

Moreover, I cannot forget my 12th-grade school counselor. In 12th grade, we had to meet with our academic counselor to go over our graduation plan and our expectations after graduation. First, let me say that I did not believe that I was a good test taker. Since this was my belief, I did horrible on standardized tests and certainly did not put forth an effort to pass them. With that said, my SAT scores were substandard!

Today, I still laugh at how I took that test. I read about 25% of the test questions, answered those questions, and guessed the answers on the rest. Now, it was time for me to meet with my counselor. During this meeting, he asked me a few questions that resulted in a hurtful statement.

Counselor: "What do you want to do after graduation?"
Me: I want to go to college.
Counselor: "Do you work now?"
Me: I found it odd, but I answered, "I work in a retail store."

Counselor: You should probably remain a cashier here in Richmond and not consider college.

Me: Radio silence! Crickets!

Me: I did what I do all the time, I hid my pain behind my smile.

This is the time that I felt the most support from my parents, as they went to that school and met with that counselor.

> **NOTE:** *As it relates to taking the SAT, I want to discourage you from doing what I did. Please, take them seriously. Start preparing for them during the 9th-10th grade so that you can pass with a high score. However, if college is not your plan, and you want to be an entrepreneur, do that! If you want to take a break after high school and work for a while, do that! Just make sure that you find what you want to do and follow that dream, not what others expect you to do.*

All these events in 5th, 6th, 11th, and 12th grade, were embedded in my computer (my mind). They manifested by me harshly judging myself in everything I did in life, work, school, and parenting. I was hard on myself.

If I did not make an 'A,' I sucked. If I thought I failed at work, I repeated that perceived failure in my mind and berated myself, i.e., "I am going to get fired!" "I can't believe I did that!" "How could I be so dumb?"

For days, I would feel horrible about my inconsistent behavior towards or for the unpleasant words I said to my children. I didn't like who I was. This leads me to the next load, but first we…

PAUSE

You must stop these negative thoughts before it becomes too difficult to come out of a self-criticizing spider web. How do you do it? You examine the evidence that may or may not support the negative self-talk.

Think of an event that is causing you to have negative thoughts and write down those thoughts. Next, find the positive evidence that negates (takes away) those negative thoughts. Then, replace those negative thoughts with the positive evidence. Find evidence that is in alignment with who you wish to become (she's already inside of there). This will allow the inner you to shine despite the opinions that surround you.

I want you to realize that the only time any failure can remain a failure is if you DO NOT get up and try again. DO NOT let failure defeat you and your inner power.

LOADING...
SELF-LOATHING

"When we don't know who to hate, we hate ourselves."
~Chuck Palahniuk from the Invisible Monster

Another helpful definition provided by Merriam-Webster's Online Dictionary is Self-loathing (hatred), which is defined as *hatred directed toward oneself rather than toward others.*

Self-hatred may be the most difficult topic for me to write about because I did not like who I was. I did not like how I looked, i.e., acne, fat (even though I was not fat), weight, etc. I did not like that I was not a good child or student. I did not like myself as a friend or an employee. I did not like myself as a wife; I hated my behaviors in my marriage. I did not like myself as a mother; my parenting skills were greatly affected. I would even hate that I hated myself.

I fought this daily, but in the end, that unseen enemy won. It was quite ridiculous how long I would stay in these valleys of hate. It caused me to try to control every event in my life. I figured that if I could make things go my way, I could recreate expectations and outcome and decrease self-loathing. Unfortunately, that did not work. It created more of what I did not want: hate and control. That unseen enemy had won again.

Controlling and being hateful can stifle us in becoming who we desire to be. It prevented me from recognizing the areas in my life that needed to be altered so that I could become better. They were blind spots, and blind spots caused me to repeat the same error until I put control and hate in their rightful place. Once I stopped resisting the beauty of all things that come out of life, the self-hate and controlling behaviors decreased. I realized what I tried to repress would always persist. In other words, the more I resisted accepting who I was, the more I prevented my true self from shining.

...the more I resisted accepting who I was, the more I prevented my true self from shining.

When I heard author Brené Brown say, "The body keeps score and always wins", I decided that I was not going to hold on to self-hate because it could manifest in other ways like in the form of a potential disease. I did not want the "unseen enemy" to cause so much dis-ease in my life that I could not love myself in peace.

PAUSE

How to stop your self-loathing/hatred? Begin by standing in the mirror. All those areas of your body that you have prejudged, and demonstrated hate towards, ask yourself for forgiveness.

Start by saying, "I am sorry that I was so "judgy" towards this beautiful body. Then ask yourself, "What will I gain from forgiving myself"? This question will cause your subconscious mind to seek a positive response.

After standing in front of the mirror, without judgment, start to journal the thoughts that come to you. Continue to do this until self-loathing is not the first reaction to your self-image or your life experience. In doing this, you are training your brain to think differently.

LOADING...
VULNERABILITY

"What makes you vulnerable, makes you beautiful."
~Brené Brown

Google defines Vulnerability as *the quality or state of being exposed to the possibility of being attacked or harmed, either physically or emotionally.*

While self-loathing was difficult to admit to the world, vulnerability is difficult to show to the world. My childhood life experiences taught me that it was not acceptable to cry or show emotions. They taught me to "suck-it-up buttercup" and keep it moving despite the pain I was feeling, seeing, or hearing. I did not want anyone to know that I was hurting; I was afraid they would use my pain against me.

If I cried, I was told to shut up. When I was emotional, no one helped me navigate those emotions. So, I pretended that all was well, and I took care of myself. This type of negative self-care led me to disregard and disconnect from what I was feeling. In essence, I was disconnecting from who I was and had hoped to be.

How did the lack of vulnerability show up for me? I perceived myself as selfish if I was vulnerable. Being vulnerable meant someone else was taking my attention. This led me to make other people more important than me, and their opinions were better for me. I thought that they were better than me and believed that my dreams were unimportant. I pursued and obtained "things" that I did not want. How does this happen, you ask?

When you emotionally disconnect from yourself, you fail to know what you like, what you want, and where you want to go. You do not recognize who you are because you have spent a lot of time not being you. Vulnerability is not only about crying; it is about taking the time to recognize that being human is a beautiful acceptance of all parts of who I am and not compartments. My mind, body, and spirit all belong together and not separate.

PAUSE

Let's go back to our computer (brain). An Information Technologist (IT) job is to keep your computer running efficiently, protecting it from, and removing any viruses. Frequently, an IT specialist will assess the system for any vulnerabilities. This involves defining, identifying, and prioritizing the functionality of the system.

You are now the IT specialist for your computer. You must define the problem, identify how the problem is impacting you, and prioritize how you are going to attack the virus (i.e., self-criticizing, people-pleasing, unworthiness, etc.) that is preventing you from being the best version of yourself.

Pull out that journal and write what vulnerability means to you (defining). After that, write down how it may be negatively impacting (identifying) your "computer" and then discover how you are going to change it (prioritizing). Vulnerability is not the enemy but rather how you perceive it is the enemy.

I end with this one last story. A young girl asked her parents for a specific pair of brand name shoes. Her parents did buy her some shoes, but not the ones she wanted. The young girl interpreted this as her parents did not love her but hated her.

Today, that young girl is a beautiful professional businesswoman who has been in several unhealthy relationships. She attended a business event, and the room was full of handsome businessmen. One businessman, who seemed to be having a lot of fun, caught her attention.

Which man did she choose as her husband?

I share this because we have to search for stories that support the initial lie that we tell ourselves. If you believe that you are unworthy, unlovable, unattractive, etc., you will have to find evidence to support that. Wouldn't you rather find stories that support positive beliefs? The good news is that you can. You get to choose, so choose wisely.

A Message to My Younger Me

Dear Younger Me,

First, I want you to know that people can only love you to the point of where their hurt and brokenness begins. Let's consider climbing a mountain. You must be prepared to climb, i.e., plenty of water, food, a backpack, and proper shoes. As you begin to ascend the mountain, you run out of the water and realize that you do not have the proper equipment to continue to the top of that mountain. So, you begin to descend from the mountain. In this case, the point you reached on the mountain is like brokenness. If their love is the extent of a half-climb, that is where their brokenness begins, and they cannot love you beyond that point. They simply do not have the proper equipment to go further. Their spirit was broken before you came into their life. They want to love beyond their hurt but can't until their brokenness is healed. Life experiences can harden the heart, so they must be willing to do the work to experience joy in life. Now that you know that you are not responsible for how that person has treated you or the harsh things they have said, you can now choose how you share your inner beauty and talents with the world. You get to choose to love you. You can take those difficult moments and turn them into whatever beauty you want. My sweet girl, you have so much to offer this world, but you have hidden behind the fears and pains of other people's opinions about you. Naw, sis! What they said was not cool; it was downright ugly. I want you to take the time to become aware of what matters to you, how your feelings impact you, and what drives you. Get to know more about what makes you angry, sad, or happy and joyful. This will bring an understanding of the intent of others and will allow you to stand in your power. Stand tall, gorgeous girl, and do as many have said, "Do not dim your light because it is too bright to someone else." One more thing, I want you to know that fear steals your joy. So, let kindness and love be your guide; they will never guide you in the wrong direction. It does not mean that you will not have difficult moments, but when you allow your heart, mind, and body to feel love and kindness, you surrender the pain. When you surrender the pain, you can return to living in your God-given power without limiting how you appear to yourself and the world. When pain and hurt start to drive your motives, your feelings, and your desires, I want you to stand in front of a mirror and do this exercise. Look into your eyes; take deep cleansing breaths through your nose, and exhale through your mouth. Tell yourself: I love you! I love you! I love you! Affirm it until the pain and hurt dissolves. At first, it may seem like it is taking forever. But the more you do it, the quicker you will shift from pain to joy and frowns to smiles. Your better-ness will begin to shine. You will recognize the power you hold, and that power cannot be torn down by anyone. It may shake you for a moment, but you will return better each time. You are perfect as you are. You are beautifully imperfect, and no one can steal that from you. You are more than enough just as you are. You do not have to be more for anyone else, but just enough for you to expect greatness from yourself. Have fun and enjoy each moment because even the painful moment will allow your pursuit of greatness will be gratifying. Please, my love, do not allow those moments to kill the dreams that are inside of you.

Beautifully made in the Image of God,
Lisa

Lauren Kelley

Lauren was born and raised in Gary, IN. She is the oldest daughter of Laurence and Vera Kelley and has a younger sister Veronica. At age 11, Lauren attended the Emerson School for the Visual and Performing Arts and majored in drama throughout middle and high school. During her time there and landed the lead role in the 2002 independent film *Posin': Know Who You Are.* Lauren holds a B.A. in Communication/Afro Studies and an MBA. She founded her first event planning company, Socials, LLC, in 2012. Catering to the creative endeavors of women and minorities led to creating an internship program and a company rebrand in 2019 - LNR Enterprises, LLC. LNR. She looks forward to the next steps in her journey, and the opportunities that being an author will provide.

Image Bearer
~by *Lauren Kelley*~

I can't pretend to know the kind of experiences you may be facing as a young woman growing up in the Social Media (SM) age. As the SM rise began right before I finished college in the early 2000s, it was still fairly innocent. It was all about connecting with family, friends, and classmates you haven't seen in a while and sharing a few pictures in the process.

Now, you have social influencers, Instagram models, trolling, and the pressure to obtain perfection in the way you look, dress, and how you spend your time. It was all about appearance, your brand, and the image you present to the world. It can also be super addictive, and very depressing when you began to compare your life to someone else's that seems much more glamorous.

That is why a recent goal of mine is to share my story, my entire story, and go "behind the curtain" of what I share on social media. I'm Lauren Nicole Kelley, the founder, and CEO, of LNR Enterprises, LLC, a company focused on highlighting the social causes, concerns, and creative endeavors of women and people of color. It took a while to craft that definition of what I do. It's a great elevator pitch and fits perfectly into my social media bio. But who am I really?

I am a daughter, sister, friend, and godmother to two beautiful girls. Even outside of these roles, I am a woman who has endured many challenges such as anxiety, a debilitating illness, struggles in my friendships and relationships, and a loss in confidence. My journey to heal and overcome these challenges involves a unique spiritual journey that I am excited to share with you. It is this journey that led to the amazing opportunity to be a co-author of Image Bearer.

I have admired Dr. Tuesday Tate from afar since I first heard her speak at my church in 2015. When she reached out to me (a perfect stranger) on social media in February 2020, I knew it was something that I was meant to be a part of. After our first conversation, she told me that my profile kept popping up while she was looking for someone else. She said she felt led by God to contact me.

Although I was extremely excited to be a part of this project, I began to realize that the subject matter of this book would challenge me like never before. I mentioned to Dr. Tate that I did not feel like parts of my story were totally mine to tell. As I read the description of some of the themes to be explored, my mind immediately entered a negative space, and I began to journey to the darkest events of my life. It was these moments that had me stuck for far too long.

Pain

My teenage years were very emotional. I was just like any other young girl trying to adjust to the changing hormones that come with the awkward transition to womanhood. Also, being a naturally emotional creature added to the rollercoaster ride during my youth. I felt a God-given ambition to strive for greatness at an early age, but it often manifested as anxiety. As a child and pre-teen, I hated feeling left behind. I remember, at the tender age of 3, begging my mom to teach me how to tie my shoes because another girl in my pre-school class knew how to tie hers.

...thwarting any unrighteous plans that I had made. My first thought was God stepped in!

My desire to keep up with those around me grew stronger the older I became. When I was in middle school, I wanted to be on my 'period' so badly because a lot of the other girls had already started. I thought that I would not be equal to them until I had started, too. The saying *"be careful what you wish for"* never rang as true in my life than it did during this time. Then, it happened. At the time, I didn't know exactly what it was. I thought that I had pooped on myself. It was on a Sunday afternoon when my family gathered at my great grandmother's house for dinner. I called my mom into the bathroom because there was this weird brown stuff in my underwear. She looked and confirmed that I had started my period. I was so excited! I felt like I had finally reached maturity. I couldn't wait to tell my cousin because she had started years earlier when she was only nine.

Several months passed before my period came again. I was beginning to think that it was a fluke. Then, one night while I was sitting on the floor eating dinner, I felt this strange pain that scared me half to death. At first, I thought it was gas. But I had never felt gas like this before. Immediately, I crouched over in pain; I was admitted to the hospital due to violent vomiting, diarrhea, and heavy blood flow. I was given these huge hospital pads to put on and it seemed like I would saturate one within minutes.

From then on at the tender age of 13, my periods came and went very infrequently, but when they did arrive, they made themselves known. I would miss at least two days of school every month, even to the point where one of my male classmates would comment to my friends "*Lauren must be on her period.*" I was mortified. I can laugh more about that part now, but nothing about my menstrual cycle has been funny.

With the guidance of my mother, I was placed on birth control at 13 to help regulate my cycle and ease the cramping that debilitated me. But nothing seemed to help. I would hover over a toilet from age 13 until adulthood. I remember having an ultrasound done in my late teens or early twenties to see if I had fibroids, but they found nothing. This went on through high school, college, and into my career. My illness began taking a toll, not only on me, but on my family as well. Especially because growing up, we shared a bathroom.

One night when I was 23-years old and still living with my parents, I was in the bathroom in excruciating pain. My dad came in and began yelling, *"WHY DON'T YOU GET UP!"* I can only imagine how frustrated he must have been by seeing me in pain month after month and wishing I were stronger. But, at that moment, I didn't want to hear him yelling at me. I wanted him to leave so that I could have some peace.

Imagine this: you are on your period, emotions all over the place, vomiting all night, terrible stomach pain, and someone yelling at you. Would you be a happy camper? I yelled at my father, and disrespectfully so, *"I KNOW ONE*

THING! YOU BETTER GET OUT OF THIS BATHROOM!" Although angry outbursts weren't uncommon in my household, this incident impacted me the most and was the biggest fight we ever had. This was devastating, because growing up, my father was a total #girldad. He took me everywhere. Throughout the years, he picked me up and dropped me off at school. He was the primary chef of the house, getting up to cook breakfast after working a night shift or double shifts at the steel mill.

Upon graduating Valedictorian of my high school class, ABC 7 Chicago invited me to be in a commercial honoring top high school graduates in the Chicago land area. My dad and I took a train ride to downtown Chicago so that I could be a part of this event. Spending that one-on-one time with my dad was one of the best moments of my life. I remember walking through the train tunnel and feeling safe navigating the big city with him by my side. As time moved on, my painful periods became a huge inconvenience on myself as well as my family. It was time to consider getting a place of my own.

Afterwards, I ran to my boyfriend's house and asked him if I could stay there while I searched for a place of my own. This was not my first choice, but I felt like I had nowhere else to go. Even though it would have been temporary, he admitted that he wasn't ready to live with someone. Although he was well within his rights to make that decision (and in hindsight, it was for the best), I felt rejected and unprotected.

Insecurity

Combining this emotional pain with the physical pain that constantly robbed me of my energy, I began a downward spiral. My confidence began to dwindle. Moreover, I endured teasing from childhood (and comments well into adulthood) about my weight. I have always been thin, but the illness, with my period, didn't help with my ability to gain weight. I became extremely insecure, which impacted my relationships. While I had several friendships during this time in my life, relationships with men other than my father suddenly became non-existent.

When it came to dating, I was somewhat of a late bloomer. I had my first boyfriend at 19. I met him when I was a GED tutor at Ivy Tech and he was a student. The relationship was toxic from the beginning, as he would run hot and cold at any given time. He would pressure me to have sex, even though I wasn't ready. Then one day, I decided I was going to do it. Although I wasn't ready, I was willing to lose my virginity to maintain a relationship with him.

I was about to leave for his house when *IT* came. That all-too-familiar crimson flow was sitting in the middle of my underwear, thwarting any unrighteous plans that I had made. My first thought was God stepped in! I called and told him the news, and to my surprise he didn't believe me. We had already gone back and forth about me not being ready, so he thought I was lying. I went to his house to talk about it and he snapped at me in front of his friends. I was devastated and our relationship ended shortly after.

I believed that not having sex is why my relationship came to an end and this contributed to my decision to lose my virginity with the next guy. We lasted for about 6-months until one day he decided to break up with me, citing my style choices as one of the reasons. He didn't like the way I dressed. Ironic, huh? After all the "undressing" I'd done for him, he didn't like the type of shoes I wore. I was heartbroken. He was my first, so that was an extra blow. My mom used to wake me up in the mornings singing Patti LaBelle's "New Day" to help me fight depression. Every morning she exclaimed, "*It's a new day!*" Thinking back, I so appreciate how she gently encouraged me to keep moving forward.

Lessons

About six months later, I met the guy who was my greatest lesson regarding relationships. It was a fateful day, November 26, 2004. I remember because it was the day after Thanksgiving. I was pumping gas, and there was a guy across from me pumping his. The pumps were moving extremely slow that day, so he struck up a conversation. He began by asking me about my car, a green Toyota Tercel. As I was going in to pay, he asked for my phone number.

Later that evening, he called me. I was in college and working on a video project in one of my African American studies classes. I decided to make a video of my family during one of our Sunday gatherings since the project's focus was on the black family. I told him about the project and that I had a camcorder that wouldn't work because I didn't have the right cord. As I was telling him this story, he asked me what type of camera I had. Lo and behold! He had the same one *and* the cord that I needed to make it work!

What a coincidence! In hindsight, I know God's hand was in us meeting one another. He sent someone to help me with my project, but I always looked at it as a sign that we were meant to be together. However, wisdom has taught me that God sends people into our lives for specific reasons and specific seasons. We must discern the difference to avoid unnecessary heartbreak.

Well at 21-years old, my discernment was *way* off. We decided to meet at *Barnes & Noble*. I took my younger sister with me for support. He gave me the cord and I was grateful for his help. I turned the project in and my professor loved the outcome. Shortly after this, we went on our first date to Olive Garden. I just knew in my heart that he was the one for me. While he was driving me home, I was all over him. By this time, it was cemented in my mind that the only way to connect with a man was through sexual expression.

As a result, I became emotionally attached to him quickly and wanted to begin a committed relationship. Unfortunately, he only wanted to be friends. I agreed, but I didn't know how deep I'd fall. Throughout the relationship, our main struggle was that we wanted different things. I had a feeling deep down in my gut, my soul that this relationship wasn't right. But I ignored it for a long time; I fought it tooth and nail. We broke up and got back together multiple times. Each time I felt more and more rejected because I wanted him. I wanted to be married

It was hard getting to know myself and define myself without a man.

to him and start a family, but he didn't want that. I still don't know if he didn't want it period or if he just didn't want it with me.

Either way, my twenties were defined by that relationship. Even after he turned me away from living with him when I needed him the most, I still hung on. When he flew off the handle about us taking Valentine's Day pictures and I asked him to help pay for them, I stayed. He was very generous, so it wasn't about the money. It was about the fact that those pictures represented a commitment that he had no desire to make.

A Journey of Healing

After seven years (I was with him from age 21 to age 28), our relationship ended. About a year later, I saw him at the mall and thought it was fate stepping in once more. Especially since it was around the same time of year that we'd met eight years prior. That evening he called me, and we discovered that we had similar things going on in our lives. For instance, I was going to the gym to gain 10-15 pounds of muscle and he was going to try to lose 10-15 pounds.

During this time, I had started my event planning business and was hosting a Christmas brunch to advertise my services. I invited him to come because I was certain that God told me that he was my husband. What I learned was that often, we hear what we want to hear when it comes to God speaking in our lives. Sometimes, we futilely try to fit what is said into what we want. Nonetheless, shortly after we reconnected, I discovered (through his lack of consistent communication) that seeing him again was about the closure I needed to move forward.

During this time, I became serious about my spiritual journey and my relationship with God. I needed to heal and find out who I was without him. This was important to me because women, in general, tend to define ourselves by the relationships we have with men. We devote a lot of time, energy, and resources to keep those relationships, and as a result, we can often lose part of ourselves.

I had some missteps along the way and started hanging out with a guy another friend of mine introduced me to. He was a big lesson because the tables were turned in that he wanted to move in with me. He started buying groceries and filling the fridge with them. I found myself in the shoes of my ex; telling him I wasn't ready for him to move in with me. This situation opened my eyes and gave me an understanding of how I had tried to move too fast, too soon with my ex. And how like my ex, I tried to use this guy for my own pleasure — that was until he told me he was celibate.

Celibate? *What is that?* I'm not sure if he was telling me the truth or if it was just his way of protecting himself from being hurt. Either way, it hit me like a ton of bricks. I had never considered this as a possibility. My relationships with men and sex had been so complicated. My first boyfriend left because I wasn't ready to lose my virginity, I stayed in relationships longer than I should because of soul ties, and now here I was trying to get it from a guy I didn't even like. I was all over the place! Somehow, at that moment, I knew that celibacy was the right option. Abstaining from sex was the missing component I needed to get me on the straight and narrow path in my quest to heal and detox.

The healing wasn't just for my sake, but to also improve the bad behaviors I had exhibited, particularly with my best friend Mia. I would often take a lot of my frustrations out on her, partly because I didn't know how to handle her transient nature, and because of my insecurities. Most of my friends were married with children and there I was single and celibate.

Although my spiritual journey was about becoming a better me, I still had a desire for marriage and family. It was hard getting to know myself and define myself without a man in my life. This was a challenge, as I was the only one in my circle who was experiencing this.

Because of this, I felt isolated and found it difficult to relate to people (both men and women). I was already insecure about being thin. As many men, particularly black men, typically prefer thicker women. However from my perspective, Mia had what men liked; she was thin on the top and thick at the bottom. My insecurities heightened around her because she got a lot of attention from men. I didn't realize until later that the attention didn't gravitate towards me because I wasn't exuding confidence.

Detour

During my celibacy journey, a lot of people didn't understand why I decided to go this route and no one I knew was taking this journey with me. I tried connecting with a woman at my church who was also on this journey, but the door never opened for a true friendship to blossom. For a long while I was alone, but with God on my side, I was able to walk this road for several years.

Somewhere along the path, I lost my way. I started thinking I was never going to meet the right guy. I tried online dating on and off throughout the years and even began dating a guy frequently for a couple of months. Although I was getting to know other people, I liked him because he was a nice person and he liked to go out and have a good time.

We went to a concert featuring *The Weekend,* went dancing, walked the mall together; it was nice to be able to just hang out with a guy and get to know him. The hard thing about online dating is you can often see when someone you've been interacting with is online. I would sometimes check to see if he'd be online after our dates and he would be. There was nothing wrong with that, but I was beginning to like him and wanted to start seeing him exclusively.

After about 4 or 5 dates, he started making sexual jokes and would ask to come back to my place. Often, in the middle of our dates, I would pray that he didn't ask me about having sex. It worked a couple of times, but eventually the joking got worse, and he was becoming frustrated. After he came to my place the first time, I had a heart-to-heart talk with him about my decision to be abstinent. Initially, he seemed cool with it, so we continued to date. Suddenly, he got very busy with work; until one day, he ghosted me.

Before his sudden departure, he said some hurtful things out of frustration. So, when he suddenly vanished, it brought out all my dormant insecurities. To fight my depression, I deleted my online dating profiles and took a solo trip to L.A. to visit my family. Once I returned, I wrote a specific prayer for the type of man I wanted: God-fearing, handsome, and talented. I even thought I met him. He was a talented, handsome videographer, and had a relationship with the Lord. I reached out to him and invited him to my birthday party. Yet, another blow! He accepted the invitation, but didn't show up. I didn't know this guy. I was only trying to get to know him, but clearly the feeling wasn't mutual.

Here we go again. I was at my wit's end. What was wrong with me?! Why couldn't I land a successful relationship?! Several months later, I ran into a guy I grew up with and there was an instant attraction. I was surprised because I had never been romantically interested in him. We flirted the entire weekend and then he began making sexual advances.

This time, I intentionally gave in. I was tired of not connecting with a man, tired of being alone on my journey; I just didn't care anymore. Although I knew this decision wouldn't necessarily change anything, I was willing to throw it all away for momentary pleasure. Unfortunately, it was more than I bargained for. After our weekend rendezvous, I reached out to him. I could tell by the way he responded that he was not interested in keeping in touch. Here I was once again, feeling used and rejected. Some people might say I was just having fun; for me, there was nothing fun about it.

I have learned that in all these situations, I still had a lot to work on within myself. I have also learned that the true nature of a man is revealed when sex is a factor. Some men would become mean and irritable when I decided to wait. And when I didn't, it was never enough to maintain a relationship because this isn't the way God intended for sex to be.

There is a level of security and comfort between two people who vow to commit themselves in marriage before God. I believe I will get there someday.

Purpose

Every day, I am working on becoming a more confident and self-assured woman. I am pushing past the insecurities that have developed throughout the years, so that I can live fully in God's purpose for my life. I am no longer staying silent about my journey and hiding behind carefully planned Instagram pictures. I own every part of my journey, the good and the bad. I am always seeking new ways to display the gifts and talents that God has freely given to me. And, in many ways, the drive I had as a little girl determined to tie her shoes is still in me.

Even today, there are many women that I am inspired by and I dream to live a life similar to theirs. However, I realize this can be a dangerous slope and can lead to comparison and depression if not channeled properly. Also, you never truly know what a person is going through behind closed doors. The glitz and glamour showcased on social media can often be a façade. This is why I was so excited to share my story.

My prayer is that you, the teenage girl or young woman who God decided needed to read the pages of this book will find insight on a different path that you can take in life. If you are feeling the pressure from a man or anyone for that matter to do something you may not be capable or ready to do, stand strong in your truth.

I believe a lot of heartache and pain in my life could have been avoided if I didn't give in to temptation: the temptation to argue, to be mean to my closest friend, and to have sex before my appointed time. I hope that you avoid temptation as well so that you bear the image of a pure vessel (2 Timothy 2:21, ESV), living a life that is pleasing and acceptable to God in all that you do (New Romans 12:1, NIV).

When the opportunity presented itself for me to be a part of this project, I had a different story in mind, one that had little to do with me in hindsight. After discussing, with my family, the direction I was considering, I realized that I have always defined myself through the experiences of other people. I now understand that I must be completely comfortable defining myself and my purpose based upon who I am, not by the relationships I currently have or will have, and not by my career.

Yes, my roots and the seeds I sow for my future business and personal relationships are important, but I realize the most important connection between my start and my finish is me. None of them could or will exist without me. So, that is where this story begins and ends. That's where yours should as well.

A Message to My Younger Me

Dear Younger Me,

One day you'll discover who you were born to be. Until then, do your best, but try not to stress out during the process of becoming. Stress can easily turn into anxiety and may be the cause of the physical pain you've experienced. So, take it easy. You've spent much of your youth worrying about some of the smallest things. It may not seem like it, now, but you are not behind. We all have our own races to run, and yours is not going to look like anyone else's. That's okay because there's only one you. I know you've struggled with feeling like an outcast. You were often the smallest person in the room and shrank yourself and played it small until you started to believe you were of little significance. Being the smallest person in a room only means you don't fit an "average" mold. You are an anomaly, and this means you were born to stand out, to "shine, beautiful sunshine" just like the first solo you sang in pre-school taught you to. You are an overcomer. No matter what struggle comes your way, you will always defy the odds and come out on top. This is just who you were born to be. You will go on to do great things: graduate top of your class in high school and college, receive two full scholarships, star in an independent film, become an entrepreneur, expand your creative ability, and be a part of an amazing book that will inspire younger generations after you. Because that's who you are, Lauren Nicole Kelley. Your very name means victory, victory of the people, and warrior. These are the images God has blessed you to bear. Love life and live it to the fullest. Go and be great! It's a new day! I love you.

Beautifully made in the Image of God,
Lauren

Desion Stewart

Desion is the eldest of four children, born in Houston, TX.

Overcoming the vicious cycle of broken relationships and marriages, single parenting, and the "night life" to accept her call as a Prophet of God has brought this young woman to many crossroads. She discovered the freedom to live a victorious life by applying God's word to her life and desires to help others do the same. She has overcome tumultuous early years to dedicate her life to helping others transform their circumstances and discover God's unique plan of destiny for their lives.

Cycles
~ *by Desion Stewart* ~

"Ya momma left you at the hospital, and they called me to take you home," my grandfather said with a smile on his face and a gleam in his eye. I replied, "Really? Daddy?" "Yeah," he responded. How was I to know he was joking; I did not remember much of what he said afterward.

My thoughts were frozen solid at the fact that she left me at the hospital. What was the reason she did not want me? What did I do? Is this why she never comes around? Is this the reason I do not know my father? If she loved me, she would have brought me home. Am I ugly? I must not belong. I cannot remember how many times I replayed those words in my mind. My grandparents were busy trying to raise us. Yes...US! Four of us; not including my brother, were raised by my grandparents. There were too many questions and feelings to deal with during that time, at the age of 6 or 7. I do remember feeling confused, angry, and sad.

Those were the only emotions I could put into words at that age. I did not know that those emotions would create wounds in my spirit, and they would live out loud in my teenage and young adult life. I needed someone to talk with, but it certainly would not be my mother. She was in and out of prison for the first 20 years of my life.

Cycles

I came to know my father's family because my maternal grandparents always welcomed his mother picking me up on the weekends. My father was an alcoholic for over 20 years of my life and died by the time I was 31. I was very much so a confused child. Most times, I felt lonely, rejected, and abandoned. These adjectives produced timidness, low self-esteem, a feeling of never being good enough, and the need for someone to love me.

I remember the times I wished my mother would come and get me like she said she would. There were other times she would promise to return and she would visit us. We would get to go with her, but those times were few in between. She always looked tired as if she hadn't slept in days. Her eyes were big and sunken in her head, which seemed extra-large. Her skin seemed "ashy" and not because she needed skin moisturizer.

There was something deeper going on. Skin and bones was her body frame, but it wasn't because she was missing any meals. She had meals, but not food. See, my mother was addicted to Crack Cocaine; that was her meal.

Neither my mother nor grandparents told me about the addiction. We lived in a small community, and neighbors were like an extended family. Everyone knew everyone, the neighbors could whoop your butt, and they talked!

The condition of my mother left me feeling ashamed, embarrassed, hurt, sad, invisible, and left out. I know that if she could have saved us from the humiliation, she would have. If she could have helped herself, she would have. I looked at her and could tell that she was remorseful and ashamed of her appearance and that she was not there for us. And more than anything, I believe she wanted to stop being an addict; but at that time, she didn't have the strength to overcome.

Many times, I cried when she left. Not only because she would be gone, for I don't know how long, but because I felt her pain. Although I wasn't aware of the depth of pain she was in, I knew it was there. The funny thing about pain (mental agony) is that you never truly rid yourself of it. You only suppress it. This suppression drives you to do unhealthier things, life-threatening things. It may not hurt as bad as it used too, but the dullness that you feel sometimes indicates that the pain is still there!

According to Current Drug Abuse Reviews, June 5, 2012, "In homes where one or more adults abuse alcohol or drugs, children are approximately twice as likely to develop addictive disorders themselves." My grandparents did the absolute best they could to raise us. There is no way we would have made it had they not stepped in. And though they were there, I ached for my mother and father's presence. I needed her touch and his words of affirmation. Being so young, I never thought that the lack of those things I wanted from them would affect me. As I grew older, I realized that it did affect me; this was the introduction to many Cycles in my life.

From my childhood to my teenage years, I was a very shy and timid girl. I struggled in reading, required extra help in class, but I learned quickly. Though I struggled academically, I had a hidden athletic ability. I was very flexible. My flexibility and being double jointed got me attention, which I liked because it made me feel loved. One day during recess, there was a gymnastic group who came to our school. When I saw how they moved, I knew that's what I wanted to be. In the back of my mind, I also knew my grandparents couldn't afford the classes. My

The funny thing about pain... you never truly rid yourself of it.

teacher, who knew of my abilities, told the instructor, and he later came and asked me to show him what I could do.

It must have been amazing to him because it earned me a free two-week scholarship. My uncle was responsible for dropping me off and picking me up. I loved every minute of it. I can still smell the air in the gym today. Walking in the place for the first time was nothing short of pure excitement. I had found where I belong. The trampolines, the uneven bars, the mats, the springboards, and OH, the CHALK!

What is a gym without chalk?! We created the clouds by slapping our hands together after plunging them into the bowl of chalk. It was exuberating. It made me feel like a real gymnast: like I knew what I was doing. Unfortunately, my dream lasted as long as my scholarship did. My grandparents couldn't afford it. It faded to black: another disappointment.

Langston Hughes' poem *"A Dreamed Deferred"* became my life's testimony.

What happens to a dream deferred?
Does it dry up like a raisin in the sun?
Or fester like a sore— And then run?
Does it stink like rotten meat?
Or crust and sugar over—like a syrupy sweet? Maybe
it just sags like a heavy load. Or does it explode?

Another feeling of, "Now where do I belong"?

Middle school years were challenging for me; I was not well liked, and I wanted to be. By whom? Boys, of course! But this was also the time you hit puberty, and your face looks like connect the zits. Oops, I meant dots. I was noodle-thin, not very shapely, and had a Jerri Curl that went wrong in so many ways. I developed alopecia, and my hair turned a burnt orange color that not even a hairstylist could duplicate. When it came to people picking teams, in our class, being teased and overlooked further solidified the negative thoughts I had about myself.

Those thoughts, coupled with not loving myself, fed my insecurities. I wanted to be like everyone who I thought was popular, cute, had a better skin tone, who was shapelier, or who had better hair. I didn't like the ME that God had created. My creative mindset led me to watch and study people. I intently watched who liked them, how they dressed, how they talked, walked, and carried themselves.

Although studying them taught me how to act, at the same time, I was learning how not to be myself. I lost my identity. I only knew that I wanted to be somebody who wanted somebody to want them.

My identity crisis led me to search where I belonged. I attended Robert E. Lee High, where I joined the school choir; soprano was my section. I also joined the marching band and played the flute. During these years, it was a predominately Caucasian school, which means so were my friends. They accepted and treated me better than my own. I got invited to many places and was involved in many programs that, ordinarily, I would not have been able to afford.

Still struggling to fit in, I thought that having a car would bring me into the "IN" crowd. My uncle bought me my first car; I was the youngest of my friends with one. Of course, this meant I was the driver when we went to clubs and parties. Even though I was underage, it didn't stop me from going. I had a friend who everyone said we look alike. So, you know what we did? She would go first with two people between us, then they would pass her ID to me, and then I'd flash it to the bouncer. I would have to tell him the date of birth (using hers) and WALLAH! I'm inside! Not only with the "right" to be inside but the right to drink!

My light drinking days started around the 9th grade with wine coolers. You can't get too much of a buzz with those. But I did like the way it made me feel. I felt very relaxed and confident. So much so that I would talk and act in ways I normally wouldn't. It was easier for me to fit in that way, under the influence. Any party where alcohol was involved, I was there. I didn't see it at the time, but alcohol would become a stronghold. It was an addiction well known on my father's side of the family. And I was headed in the same direction as this family curse.

I loved the club life but could only do it if I had some strong alcohol. When I walked through those doors, with liquor in me, I was a different person. I was BOLD! CONFIDENT! You couldn't tell me nothing! When the DJ knew I was in the building, he played my song. I paraded around with a drink in my hand and headed to the dance floor. With my 'can't tell me nothing attitude,' I danced with whomever and drank whatever. I thought everybody wanted me and wanted to be me. Tuh! The epitome of vanity!

However, with my drinking came the attention of Men! MEN! And MORE MEN! Looking back, I shake my head at my younger self, saying, "Girl, if you only knew what was up ahead!" I only wanted to date light-skinned guys; his hair didn't matter, though. LOL! And he had to be tall and medium built. He had to have a car, the kind with the hydraulics and sound system so loud it could throw your heart rhythm off, and he could not be in high school. Preferably, he would be in college or have a steady and well-paying job. He couldn't dare be living at home with his momma!

So, if he met all of those criteria, still shaking my head at my younger self, I would give him a chance. Personally, those were viable standards. Now, he had to be able to "woo" me; remember, it didn't take much because I was starving for attention, affection, and love. To me, when he met the criteria, he was "the one." The one? Yeah! I would give my heart, my thoughts, my love, and my body to the one. Well, this standard became a repeat cycle because several guys met my criteria, and the one became too many! Everyone seemed to be "the one."

Hanging out in the clubs created another deep hole in my heart. I was in and out of relationships, and in and out of beds hoping FOR the "right one." This hopping around created and solidified self-doubt. Questions flooded my mind: Does anybody want me? Does anybody see how good I am? How reliable and caring I am? How loving and beautiful I am? Much of me believed if he couldn't see how good I was for him, maybe I could convince him by sleeping with him. Many club excursions led to one-night stands, hoping that I would find a man who meets my needs. And God knows I had many of them - one-night stands.

The false image I created about me made me believe I had enough power to persuade a man to do whatever I wanted him to do, especially when intimacy was involved.

Now you have to remember that I was full of vanity and a legend in my mind! When you have issues as I had, you tend to look for someone to fix you or to meet unrealistic - and sometimes unhealthy - needs. Isn't it interesting that I convinced myself that I could get a man to be mine, but I could not change my mind about myself?

I always thought I knew what I wanted, but it changed with almost every man who came into my life. I was broken into millions of pieces and didn't realize how lost, scattered, and shattered I was. How can you put a broken person together? Have you ever noticed the many broken pieces of a cup or plate? Be sure to include the fact that some pieces shatter to dust. Have you ever tried gathering up the pieces; the fine particles with the jagged edges? When you glue them together, you can still noticeably see the lines and the cracks. Someone sees it and may think that something used to belong there.

But what? Dust! What remains is dust. While gathering up the fragments, you run your fingers across the broken cup and wipe the dust off your hands. No amount of glue is enough to put the cup back together. There will always be evidence of the breaks and cracks; depending on how deep the break is, the cup, still leaks.

This illustration is much like how my life used to be, so many broken pieces. There we so many cracks where dust-like particles were missing. All the glued cracks resulted in leaks! Leaks in me caused me to be more fragile. With every break, I came to a place where I was completely damaged.

Broken and not fixed

In my brokenness, I was still able to function - somewhat; I was still able to work. We once owned a daycare, and I would watch the children play with the toys. There were a few toys badly broken, but they loved them and continued to play with them. I didn't see anything wrong with the broken toys and whole toys mixed in the same toy bin until, one day, the Lord showed me how they were playing as if every toy was well put together. With so many emotions, sad, hurt, and amazed, I watched them play for hours. I remember there was a grocery basket missing a wheel; they would still push it.

...being damaged is a whole lot different than being broken.

One child even placed cardboard underneath the missing wheel to push it more efficiently across the floor. It was at that moment I saw my brokenness, but still functioning as if there was nothing wrong. I found other things to substitute what needed repairing. I learned how to live within my brokenness, not realizing it was causing me, and others in my life, damage. And being damaged is a whole lot different than being broken!

While living the club life, I thought I could meet "Mr. Right." I thought we would settle down and live a good life and have children. I thought he would help with the children I already had, but that never came to pass. Instead, it was just more brokenness, disappointment, and loneliness. The drinking got worse, and I started to experiment with drugs that some neighbors introduced me to. Too afraid to try anything too hard (remembering what it did to my mother), I only smoked weed and Chronic; they were my stress relievers. At first, it was free; but that was a setup. Eventually, I had to buy it. By the grace of God, I didn't become an addict; but I was jonesing for it.

I soon left Houston and moved to California with an ex-boyfriend's mother who loved me even after her son and I broke up. Coming out of failed marriage number two, and a young mother with three children, she wanted to help me start over. I was not a stranger to Cali, but this time I needed to do things differently. Unfortunately, those good intentions didn't last long. One night, I got invited to a block party, and it was all the way LIVE! Much drinking and smoking were going on. I mean if you didn't smoke the second-hand smoke guaranteed a contact high. I joined in and was doing what everyone else was doing.

Soon, I found myself having an out-of-body experience. God spoke to me and told me that the things I was feeling in my body were because I was going into cardiac arrest. He asked me if I wanted to live, and if I did, I needed to quickly ask the young lady for a cold cup of water to drink. I did, and she gave it to me. I quickly drank it and went to the restroom, where the Lord told me that my life was headed for an end if I didn't change my ways.

He also told me He had a purpose and plan for my life, but because I had always put other things and other people first, I continued the wrong path. He said I needed to repent and ask Him to save me, and He would not only give me eternal life, but He would show me my purpose and prepare me for it.

I told God I wanted to live, and I would give my life to Him if I could have another chance. So, I went back to Houston to get my car because I was offered a job in California. They allowed me a week to gather my things, tie up loose ends, and start work.

New Beginnings

I cried out to Him in my place of despair. He said, *"If you allow ME to heal you, and you do what I tell you, this pain you feel you will never feel again. But you must do it my way."* I want to tell you it was a journey. The Lord instructed me to get in the shower so that He could talk to me. Water has always been a place where I can hear the voice of God, and as I begin to bathe, it felt as if years of dirt and filth were coming off me. My first instruction was for me to fast for 40 days. The first time I heard God say it, I knew I heard wrong.

After three days of coming to God in prayer and Him telling me the same thing, I finally yielded. I ate soup once a day, no meats, no dairy, no sweets, no juice, no bread, and no snacks. He even told me what music I could listen to and no television. My daily routine during my fast consisted of going to work, coming home to my children, spending time with God in worship and prayer. I had no company in my apartment unless it was my mother and close friends from church.

My social outlet, if you call it that, was church. And I didn't give my number to anybody, especially men, and had no contact with them either. Reading Ephesians 4:27, I was determined to do this God's way in order not to repeat cycles. The life I was living required me to be disciplined by

God. I had to be willing and obedient for these cycles in my life to be broken and destroyed. I had to give myself a chance to be made whole.

Likewise, you must be willing and obedient to participate in your healing for the cycles in your life to be broken and destroyed, and for you to be made whole. Too many times, we want what God says is ours, but we are not willing to do what He said to get it. You may think my life or journey was strict and strenuous, but the rewards are endless. While others were still living and getting the same results from it, I chose to leave the lifestyle that broke me. I knew I had to consecrate myself and become serious with God. Luke 9:23 says, *"Whosoever wants to be my disciple must deny themselves, take up their cross daily, and follow me."* This was my desire.

I had to ask the Holy Ghost to help me not to crave the things I was used to doing and having. I didn't know how to be friends with the opposite sex without having sex. So, I had to learn how to be friends with men without wanting them as lovers. These were the very things that were killing me softly. Looking fine as wine on the outside, but full of dead men's bones on the inside. Paul said in Romans 7:24, *"Oh wretched man that I am who will deliver me from this dead body."*

Are You Ready?

Can you see the cycles? Wanting to be loved, looking for love in all the wrong places by jumping into so many relations: not taking time to heal before I met the next person, and got sexually involved with them. Clubbing because I knew I could meet the right person this time: moving from one place to another with no stability. Alcohol and drug use to deal with my inner pain. Can you relate? By now, many thoughts of your childhood may be revisiting your mind and heart.

Can you feel what I felt? Can you sense the little girl's hurt, shame, disappointment, and loneliness? Can you hear her crying? Can you see you are where I once was? Of course, you can, but this time, I encourage you not to run from your pain but face it so you can heal. Feel the fear and do it anyway so you can be healed. I cannot stress enough that your healing is solely up to you being a willing and obedient participant. Isaiah 1:19 says, *"If you be willing and obedient. You will eat the good of the land."*

Many are obedient but not willing, meaning they will do a thing, but in their soul and spirit, they are defiant; they grumble and complain. This type of mindset will delay what God wants to do for you and give to you. An 11-day trip for the children of Israel turned into a 40-year experience because they were disobedient and unwilling to submit to and obey God. They were not willing to believe and do what God told them about the promise of the land He was sending them to.

Take this time to reflect. What are you unwilling to do or obey? What are you fighting about or arguing about with God? You must be honest with yourself and blame no one else or anything else another day. You must be willing to take accountability for where and why your life is and the place that you are in today. I could have gone on and on with reasons and blame others as to why my life was topsy-turvy. But the common denominator was and is me. The first step to recovery is owning the works of your hand that has stifled you. This step is one of the most painful steps in recovery. But just like birthing a child, although it hurts, it also brings astonishing joy, hope, and completion.

Being obedient to God is vitally important. I believe it protects us from the adversary, the devil. Look at Job. The Bible said he was a perfect man, upright and shunned evil (Job 1:1). Even though he did no wrong, he still faced and went through challenges, losing all he had. But the very thing Job needed (God), protected his soul from Satan. His obedience warranted protection. So, don't count what God is telling you as too small or insignificant, and you willingly disobey. You must conclude that you are ALL-IN no matter the cost.

So, how do I do that? I stayed away from people, the friends I used to club with, smoke with, and drink with, who were still struggling. They would tease me about my commitment to change, saying it doesn't take all that, or you're just a "goody-two-shoes" or a "holy-roller". They saw me like this because I decided not to smoke, drink, and sex my hurt away, anymore. By no means did I think I was better than them, I just wanted something different. And to get that something, I had to set boundaries.

First Corinthians 15:33 reads, "Be not deceived: evil communications corrupt good manners." Setting and upholding boundaries is a wonderful thing. To me, it meant I no longer had to prove anything to anyone anymore. Establish your boundaries, respect them, and demand that others do the same. Boundaries are there for your protection, safety, and peace of mind, don't remove them for anyone!

Set a standard and don't settle because you feel that nobody will want you because you have children, you look a certain way, you don't have a certain thing or you should be further than where you are. How do you know you should be further? By whose ruler are you measuring up to? If it's because you're looking at others, then your measuring stick is up against the wrong person. God only knows. (Prov 19:21, Psalm 119:133-136)

Many times, the enemy will have you comparing yourself to others. Comparison is a slow death; it kills. It kills your peace, the your hope, things that make you unique, and more. Psalm 139:14 reminds us to praise God for how we are made, *"I will praise thee; for I am fearfully, and wonderfully made: marvelous are thy works; and that my soul knoweth right well."* Being that my life was full of drama, stress, secrets, games, scandals, and lies, I didn't think I had much peace in my earlier years. Shoot! Looking back: there was no peace. I have come to love peace. I have learned to not to compare and strive. With all due diligence, fight for the peace that is yours.

Identify when a relationship is only platonic or meant to be romantic. If it is causing you to lose valuable time, sleep, joy, things, and happiness, it's too expensive; and chances are you will not have peace, and that is not worth it. Remember the brokenness of my mother? And how it affected our relationship? Well, my mother gave her life to Christ and was delivered of her drug addiction and has been free for over 27 years now. Our relationship is as how it should have been, but I cherish it so much more because of where it's been. She's been a support system for me when I've gone through my darkest times.

It's Your Time

By now, there may be some emotions that have stirred up in you. If that is so, then you are in the place I prayed you'd be. I hope that as you read this chapter and book, the healing power and deliverance of God would meet you right where you are. Understand that what you have felt from the moment you began to read this book is preparing you for a successful move into the next season of your life. It's good that you are feeling what you are feeling. These emotions make room for God to come in and do the work. And what might the work be, you ask?

Well, one is learning how to love yourself: even the parts of you that you are not particularly crazy over. Treat yourself to a movie. Not with your friends! You, and only YOU! Take yourself to dinner, not a fast-food drive-thru place, but a fancy sit-down dinner. Imagine! Dream! Dress up as you would if you were going on the best date ever! Treat yourself, as you would want the man of your dreams to treat you.

Make a list of 100 things that you want to accomplish in life. It doesn't mean you have to complete them all, but it will motivate you and help you not become complacent. Complacency breeds stagnation, and stagnation births death; death to your hopes and dreams. Keep a journal to document what you have achieved. Train yourself to write every night. If you're not a writer, take out your phone and record your thoughts. I do both and have done it for years. When you read your journal or listen to your recorded thoughts, you will discover how much you've matured or where you need to improve.

You've been in the darkness for far too long, carrying the weights of shame, guilt, anger, bitterness, and unforgiveness. And although I do not discount the pain and the depth of what you're feeling, I know that God is more than able to bring you on the other side of it. Does this mean that afterward, your life will be filled with roses and on the up and up? No, it does not.

First of all, I want you to know you are not alone and there is always help for you. I recommend that you find a support group or visit a local church that can equip you with the powerful tools to survive and overcome every obstacle, every challenge, every trial in your life because you are not alone. I know, I know, I can hear some of you, "Oh, that's so corny!" Inside all of us, there is a small voice that we can hear with clarity if we take the time to be still and listen. God is not a myth; He's not a fairytale; He is not the man upstairs. He is your Father, who created and formed you in your mother's womb.

And God is better than the ones who brought you into the world. Even if you have not yet received His Son Jesus, He is still your Heavenly Father, and Jesus is still the Savior of the world, and that includes you. The One who can deliver you out of every jam you find yourself in: He is God and God alone.

Get to know God more intimately. How do you do that? By going to church, spending time with Him in prayer, and reading and studying His Word. Make God your priority. Set aside quiet time to hear from the Lord; whether it is first thing in the morning (which is probably best and a great way to jump-start your day), midday, or in the evening before bed. The goal is to make time for God as you would for the one you love or your best friend. Do you know how it feels when you are a special one or are number one in someone's life?

These feelings cause you to believe that this person genuinely loves you and that they'd do anything for you. Now, imagine God feeling this way because He's number one in your life. I challenge you to take the step to open up and let Him in. Why? Because you need deliverance from years of pain and misery and without Him, life will continue to be the same as it has been. And, who needs this type of life, when He sent His only begotten Son that you may have a more abundant life? To God be Glory! Welcome to your new life of abundance!

A Message to My Younger Me

Dear Younger Me,

There are so many things I want to tell you that will help you along this journey called life: a lot of things that will save you from a lot of heartaches, disappointment, and pain if you will receive, listen, and follow-through. I know you want to fit in and be liked by your peers. But popularity at such a young age is, at times, overrated. Love who you are. I know it may seem awkward because you stand out like a sore thumb - so tall, so thin, so quiet, and timid. But I need you to know that you are so incredibly unique and beautiful. So much so that many do envy you. Oh yes! You do not see it right now, but it is the truth! Of course, they will never tell you, but they know there is something very different about you. Don't let your indifference cause you to feel inferior; you are not second-class! Every morning and night write at least two affirmations for the next 21 days. For example, I am bold. I am beautiful. I have no fear of speaking to anyone about anything. Say this to yourself while looking in the mirror. And look into your eyes and say it: not at your lips. Make the connection as you speak to yourself and allow yourself to see you from the inside out. Trust me; this will change how you see yourself and value yourself. It will build a wall when people try to tell you things that you know are not true about yourself. I know there will come a time when you will like boys and want them to like you. I want you to know who you are and love you first. Those affirmations I told you about, they will help in this area. Look in the mirror and tell yourself how good you look. Tell yourself how that outfit looks good on you. Can you see it? Can you see how good you look? Doesn't that outfit make you feel great? Yeah! That's what I'm talking about! I can see the smile on your face as you read and imagine this. Don't let your imagination and your dreams die. And speaking of dreams, start your own business without fear. Remember, you are unique in many ways. And *dreaming of starting your own business is not a far-fetched dream. Even if people disagree with you, PURSUE IT! GO AFTER IT! It is YOUR dream! Let me add an affirmation here: People come to me because I have what they need, and they have what I need. People from all over the world are looking for me because I have what they need. You have no idea of the connections you are making, and doors that will open because you believe in yourself. I used this affirmation many times and can't tell you of the divine connections that came from it. Sometimes when it happened, I honestly forgot that I even said such things, which leads me to tell you this. I only wish I had done it years early on. Start making dream boards. Get some of those magazines you have and cut out pictures of where you want to live, the house, the car, and the career. Paste them on a board or in a notebook, somewhere on the wall where you can see it every morning and every night before bed. I want you to look at what you have put together for your life. Look at it! Feel it! See yourself living it and begin to thank God for it! Remember, there is power in your* thoughts, which turn into words. So be careful of what you think and say. Don't allow negative people to stay in your personal space. Guard your heart. Your time and friendship are valuable. You don't have to go along to get along. Above all, make time for God. Spend time with Him daily. Pray and read the bible. I know you will be tired by the end of the day but make it your business to talk to Him. Ask Him to direct your path. Ask Him for wisdom and discernment because you will need them. Don't think of Him as someone who is in a far-off galaxy, or who is a thing. He is a Spirit, and He created you. He knows everything about you. So, if there be a time you don't understand yourself or anything else, ask of the Lord. He will answer you. For the times you are feeling down, or are brokenhearted, know that there won't be pain all your days. Learn from the experience and be quick to forgive and let go. Don't let your failures cripple you; for without them, there is no reason to strive for success. Don't silently speak negative thoughts of what you think you didn't do right or well. It will only set you back, hinder, and undermine your growth in *every area. Cry when you need to cry and move on. Don't stay in a place of hurt for too long; it poisons your ground (heart), makes life hard, and makes dreams even harder to come true. Finally, I love you. You will have a successful life. You are a leader, and many will follow you. Everything you've ever dreamed of will be yours. Don't delay it by getting involved with people and things that don't have your best interest. Your future will be long and fruitful. Always be kind, helpful, and love people. Don't wait for others to appreciate you and buy you things. Love yourself; date yourself; treat yourself. I want you to know that you are blessed and can never be cursed. You are the head and never the tail. You are above only and never beneath. And because God is the greatest power, you will never be defeated.*

Beautifully made in the Image of God,

Desion

Dr. Tuesday Tate

Tuesday is the CEO of ATK Speakers and Publishing (ATKSP) Firm and is the Executive Editor of the publishing arm of the firm. She is a multi-facet, progressive, and consummate professional as the CEO of both Vision Focus Group World Wide (providing Strategy and Certified Training and Coaching Services) and T. Tate Ministries International. She effectively uses her talents, gifts, skills, and knowledge as an ordained Prophetic Minister, motivational speaker, certified coach and trainer, author, publisher, and media personality to help individuals and organizations identify, document, and achieve their goal. She is charged and elated to be living her life's purpose and helping others do the same.

Fearfully Made
~by Dr. Tuesday Tate~

The image of God is distinct. Though His image is glorious; it is not focused on physical beauty, it is spiritual and everlasting. Wisdom of Solomon 2:23 records, *For God created man to be immortal and made him* (human beings) *to be an image of His own eternity.* The righteous (believers in Jesus) can rest in the full hope of eternal life because God made them in His image.

> *"Oh my God, what have you done... Why would you cut yourself...?" Minister Tate, she cut herself...! She's been cutting herself...!"*

As I raced to the thirty-six hour watch-ward of the hospital, I pondered the severity of her action and more importantly, the hopelessness of her heart to choose to, try to, and want to harm herself and end her life. There are so many of our young people and more specifically, our girls and young women who; for different and similar reasons have had or are battling with thoughts of suicide. And to drill down even more, our African American teens and young women's challenges are even more intense. According to PBS News recorded October 18. 2019 it states that for every 100,000 youth ages 10-24, close to 11% (10,000+) of those deaths were due to suicide – self-murder. Though adolescent self-reported attempts and plans have dropped; the suicidal attempts and successes among African American youth have increased by 73%. Why? Why is this permanent solution to a temporary issue easier than finding someone to talk to in-order to resolve it?

The article goes on to say that racism; poverty, community crime, hunger, and police-involved shootings, etc. may be the driving forces behind the self-murder increase. Similarly, the LA Times showed in a June 18, 2019 article that "for girls and young women, the suicide rates have followed a steady upward trajectory since 2000, roughly doubling between then and 2017."

Truth is youth, all youth, but specifically, African American youth need access to mental health treatments. Long before drug or substance abuse, or acting out, were other signs of depression: being sad, low in spirit, unable to concentrate, loss of appetite, change in friends, and social activities are also significant signs of depression and should be taken seriously.

As an ordained minister, I may step on some toes with what I am about to say. Because historically, African Americans have relied primarily on the church and prayer to overcome mental illness, including depression and suicidal thoughts, we have ignored, avoided, and made therapy and medicine taboo.

This taboo has not only harmed and hardened our adults, but it has also pigeonholed our youth. Young people who may live with someone who has mental dis-ease and who themselves may be struggling with it e.g., depression or suicidal thoughts. Having a mental illness or dis-ease does not mean you are crazy. It simply means you need help to deal with and manage your day-to-day life challenges.

To my teens, "tweens," young and older women, as an ordained minister of this glorious full Gospel of Jesus Christ, I encourage and release you to seek and get professional, therapeutic, preferably Christian counseling. There is nothing wrong with, taboo, or weak about you getting professional counseling. God has doctors who practice medicine and prescribe tools and resources to facilitate your healing. Up until recently, I had a therapist. She was on speed dial! Listen, I will acquire one again if I deem it necessary.

Though I believe that the church, prayer, fasting, and therapy are essential to our healing, deliverance, and freedom; the most vital part of all of this is God Himself. From a dark waiting place and space called a womb, i.e., from your mother's uterus, God made, formed, and fashioned you.

HE brought you forth in His image and likeness. And HE did this because of, out of, and from *Love.* The most important thing you can do is to receive, accept, and understand that God loves you. HE loves you so much that if it were just you, HE would have sent His son Jesus to die for you and Jesus would have accepted the call because you are just that important to Him and them.

Who told you that?

In Genesis 3, God asked Adam, "Who told you, you were..." I submit this same question to you. Who told you what you believe about God and yourself? What caused you to not believe in yourself? To ask God why HE made you a particular way is an unhealthy learned behavior that often comes from childhood and creates a sense of insecurity and unworthiness.

Who told you that you were that or that you cannot do or be that? Who did this to you? What situation brought you to this place in your life? Who told you, 'you do'n too much' when all you're trying to do is God's will and live your purpose? Who told you that you could not have it all? Who told you your African American features were not beautiful, not accepted; you or they had to be changed, modified, or erased? Who told you black was not beautiful? It was around middle or high school that I started asking myself and probably others, "If our black is so unattractive or unaccepted, why were those of a lighter hue (white people) always trying to get darker and getting skin cancer doing it? Why are they putting stuff in their lips and behind so they could be full or bigger like ours...?" Things that make you go, "Hmm...."

I was somewhere between 12 and 14 years old and heard something I had never heard before. I was at my childhood church in Benton Harbor, MI, Union Memorial AME Church, and we were hosting our Regional Conference. My Pastor, Delano L. Bowman, had an effective way of engaging the youth. For most of us, he was more of a father or grandfather than a Pastor. He had taken an interest in me, and I had started helping the church secretary, Ms. Lovey. Boy, those were fun times. Little did he and I know; well, probably I was the only one who didn't know, that today I would be serving the church through the ministry of God's Word. *Anywho*, back to the conference.

I needed to know why I was not pretty.

170

Pastor Bowman took a moment out of a busy morning and introduced me to the Presiding Elder. The Presiding Elder said, "Aren't you a pretty girl...such distinct African features..." Well, at that age that meant nothing to me. Was that supposed to be a compliment?

At that time, all I knew of Africa was the made for TV movie "Roots", jungles, unkept hair; what I considered unattractive people (women) because that is what they showed us and how they presented them on TV in the '70s and '80s. Our culture and communities were still pitting the dark-skin and light-skin, good hair (which equaled long hair) and bad hair (which equaled short and "nappy") against each other. Unfortunately, this currently happens.

What complicated this whole thing was around that time, my father bust my little bubble and told me that I was ugly. Well, he didn't say that specifically, but that's how I heard it. Teased in elementary because of my nose, lips, and yes, my African features; in all honesty, I wanted nothing to do with it. Years later, while in college, I went on a search. Why do we (I) have a broader nose, bigger booties, fuller lips, and tighter curls that we as African Americans unaffectionately refer to as "nappy"; I needed to know why I was not pretty.

I was in my late 20s before I grew to like my African features. That is a long time to exist in this body of me – ten years old starting my cycle, puberty, adolescence, boys and "boy-friends," men, and "man-friends" who we still called boy-friends – for me not to like who I was and how God made me. In my early development, I had a very shapely body that I knew not its purpose. I put my focus on the wrong assets and allowed males to do the same. A body with no understanding of its value can be a dangerous thing. We perish for lack of knowledge and boy it was definitely satan's plan that I perish!

I did not know my value, worth, or beauty, and no one was affirming me as a girl or young lady. Smart, yes attractive, but able to be whatever I dreamed was not standard conversation. In an off-handed way, I was told I should be a lawyer because I like to talk and argue. Interesting, I heard and accepted that and was on my way to law school before God called me into ministry. But with the information I had about me that I saw as "fact", what do you think I did...? Yep, unfortunately I went with what I knew. By the time I was in middle school, I knew I had a fierce body, but I didn't understand that I was beautiful or made by God!

And who was supposed to tell me that? My mom, my father, my siblings, my teachers, my pastor, myself, boys?

Before that day, with the greeting of the Presiding Elder, I do not believe I had ever heard it said to me or about me that I was beautiful, unique, or different in a positive and good way. Let me stop here and speak to parents; specifically, fathers.

> **NOTE:** *You must instill in your daughters their worth and value; it is imperative! If you don't, the world will... Boys and men who may mean them no good will. If you don't tell your daughter that she is beautiful, smart, and can do and be whatever she wants, and if you don't build her up, someone else will. And again, most often that someone will be a boy and her peers. Often that looks like peer-pressure to be something they are not to be accepted and or to fit in. For different reasons, you must also encourage your sons as well. If for nothing more than telling them that God created them to be kings, and they will one day be men who are purposed to lovingly lead their community and family and be a great husband and father.*

Leading with what I thought were my best "assets" opened the door to heart and headaches. Though God made me fearfully (awesomely) and wonderfully, I had no clue that included and encompassed my purpose, intelligence, sense of humor, creativity, sense of style, caring heart, loyalty as a friend, and His greatness in me. Being amazing is what God created, formed, and fashioned me (and you) to be, but no one had ever told me that.

Perhaps, they did not tell me of my greatness because they did not know it about themselves or me. Or maybe because they were African-Americans born in the 30's that had been (directly or indirectly, verbally, and non-verbally) conditioned to be modest and not vain and raised in an era that they were not seen as equal to others. Perhaps they were taught not to be prideful or conceited and not think highly of themselves. To think like this would mean you were haughty, high-minded, or you thought you were better than or equal to others.

These implanted mindsets of unworthiness and inequality come from slavery, Jim Crow, and segregation. Thinking or speaking positively of themselves was being high-minded, prideful, and maybe even dangerous. This existed well into the 70s and 80s and depending on where you lived or traveled, you may see it today in how people live, think, interact, and oppress others. The post-slave experience did not allow us to look white people in the eye, speak to them first, to walk in front of or alongside them, to sit with, beside or upfront, or to go into a building before them. Unfortunately and unknowingly too most, post-traumatic-slave-syndrome is real. And many (older) African Americans and Caucasians still have a slave mentality, mindset, and mind-mats.

What is wrong with knowing you are beautiful, gifted, and talented? What's wrong with having pride in yourself, family, heritage, grades, talents? What's wrong with valuing yourself with standards and boundaries? Nothing! Absolutely, nothing! Often, as Christians and "positive thinkers", we live a life of contradictions. We sing songs of how great God is, we read and quote scriptures of on how awesome HE is and His purpose for us. We hold on to and post sayings of great speakers and leaders and do our daily affirmations and meditations. Yet, we are afraid to be and walk in what HE says about us. Why? We are afraid to be great! Yes, great!!! God is great and God is in you and me. Which means you and I have The Greatest of All Times and His greatness in us. We are GREAT! HE is waiting on us – on you to "be" and walk in your greatness.

Often when a young person or a young woman; (anyone) is confident in themselves and in God, they will be labeled as prideful, worldly, controlling, vain, or a demanding female or they will be accused of *"doing too much"*. This labeling is very damaging and can break the spirit and progression of those God has called to advance His Kingdom.

For many years this was my struggle. I had not connected to His greatness in me. I had not grasped that HE who is sovereign, formed me in His image and likeness and said that I was wonderfully made. As a young girl and woman, and sometimes into my adulthood, it was not acceptable or welcomed for me to be who and all God had created and called me to be! Often I did not know how or where I fit in. From I young age, I knew or understood stuff I should not know or relate to. My father would say I came out grown... because I "acted" grown. Child's face, woman's body, adult mindset... a lethal combination. Growing up into my 20's, frequently I was the youngest person in my group. Running with 30 and 40 year olds resulted in me often dating men who were older than me. Though Psalms 139 was preached and taught to me and God was exalted as the Great I Am; neither was ever used to empower me. I would venture to guess that this is true for most and many adults.

I had allowed the weight to attach itself to me because I was hiding.

Own It

Every earthly father provides the seed that determines the unique makeup of the child, and the mother provides the incubator to house and protect the child until it's time for him/her to come into the world. Yet have you ever looked at your parent or parents and not saw yourself? Or maybe at one stage of your life, you looked like your mom and another like your dad? Or, you may have thought, "I don't see either of them when I look in the mirror." Who do I resemble? People will say, "Oh, you look just like your dad (at that age), or you look like your mom." "Ok, thank you, but I don't see it. What are they seeing? The image I see looking back at me is not the same as my father or mother." Well, beloved, I have your answer.

Though your mom and dad came together to conceive you, it was God who created and formed you in His image (Genesis 1:27). And that image is one of love, power, and beauty! Psalm 139 reminds us that God created us and His creation of us was breathtaking and wonderful. Can you, are you willing to believe what God said and is still saying about you? Are you open to believing in Him and believing Him? Can you accept His Word and thoughts concerning you and then choose to walk in them, and rest in His beautiful image of you, His purpose and plan for you and your life?

I remember the first time I looked in the mirror and said, "I like you." I was 45-years old. Yes, 45! Sometime before that, I had committed to loving me. Now, my commitment was to love me enough to like me and choose me. One of the ways I did this was to lose 60 pounds before my 45th Birthday. By God's grace, I did it! With no griddle or body shaper, I could see my waste. It was during this journey that God revealed to me that I had allowed the weight to attach itself to me because I was hiding, hiding from the world and myself all His wonderfulness in me. Not wanting to be perceived or labeled as vain, prideful or arrogant. Not wanting to be rejected; in fear, I hid behind false humility.

HE allowed me to see and face the truth that I had hidden my fierce size 12/14 behind a fashionable size 16/18. Subconsciously, I had remembered all too well the trouble I got in with that size 12/14. I had not chosen me; to own all of me; my nose, my thighs, my stomach, my lips, my hips, my backside, my hair. Why would I not with my African features? Why? *Because* I didn't like me. I had grown to love me, but I did not like what I saw in the mirror. You do know it's possible to love you and others, and not like you or others? Though my plus size did not stop brothas from approaching, it kept me from receiving.

I was traveling, ministering the Word, making educational strides, completed my first book collaboration, launched the Father Loss Forum Ministry for men, and the list goes on. Yet, my achievements were not enough for me! At times, I felt unappreciated, incomplete, limited, held back, unworthy, overlooked, etc. These words and feeling would probably shock people because nothing about me spoke this. Which shows that internal feeling or thoughts exist but not control you but in some way they will limit you and keep you from soaring. Was any of it the truth? Yes and No.

Early on it was me in my immaturity; my lack of confidence, my insecurity, my youth that fostered these feels. As the years went by and these traits faded because of truth and power, being amazing and exceptional was applauded, but not fanned. Fanning the flame of the gifts and talents given to me by God meant taking flight and modifying others access and availability. It also meant leaving others and my own comfort zones. Taking flight meant going higher and soaring. Soaring meant leaving and advancing beyond where I was. Though it was never directly spoken for me to stay low and mediocre, soaring was not encouraged or promoted. I recall comparing my state to a plane that had taken flight and got up in the air at 30,0000 feet, but had not broken through to its next level; its highest height. I was now hovering over a destination, not going higher or able to successful land. What was this...? It was me not freeing myself from others thoughts, opinions, and words and letting me be all of me.

Given permission or not, I had to decide to break formation and the ranks of tradition and limitation and climb higher and soar! Marianne Williamson says it like this, "Our deepest fear is not that we are inadequate. Our deepest fear is that we are powerful beyond measure. It is our light, not our darkness that most frightens us. We ask ourselves, 'Who am I to be brilliant, gorgeous, talented, fabulous?' Actually, who are you and I not to be? You (we) are a child of God; playing small does not serve the world. There is nothing enlightened about shrinking back so others won't feel insecure around you. We are all meant to shine. We were born to make manifest the glory of God that is within us. It's not just in some of us; it's in everyone. And as we let our own light shine, we unconsciously give other people permission to do the same. As we are liberated from our own fear, our presence automatically liberates others."

Finally, ready to say yes to my future and my success; I got sick of others and my own minimalism; their limited thinking, pocketed mustard seed faith, and my self-imposed fears and unrealistic expectations. I canceled my membership to mediocre and ran full on towards God's purpose and plan for me. Chains, bolts, and locks that imprisoned my mind began to break. False burdens, pre-conceived false notions, and negativity began to dissipate. With all boldness and confidence, I started to own and accept my stuff: the truth that God had gifted me in multiple ways. HE has commissioned me to go and positively influence, impart, encourage, and inspire others, including men.

Owning and accepting God's truth about me and His love for me freed me to use my talents and gift, brilliance, and beauty (inside and out) for the purpose God created me for was the least I could do. And guess what dear heart, HE is waiting and expecting you to do the same. Whether you are 12, 15, 21, 29, 56 and beyond, decide today, right now; I am going to be who and what called me to be. I am fearfully and wonderfully made. I am His grand workmanship. I am God blessed image in the earth.

The Scripture says in Ephesians 4:11-13 that Christ gave gifts (in the way of people) "...to *equip His people for works of service, so that the body of Christ may be built up until we all reach unity in the faith and in the knowledge of the Son of God and become mature, attaining to the whole measure of the fullness of Christ."* As it was for me not to use my talents and spiritual gifts, and to not allow God to present me as a gift that is acceptable to Him was irresponsible and selfish of me and so I would be the same for you.

EXERCISE

Do you value you? Do you appreciate you? Do you like you? Look in the mirror (clothed and then unclothed) at the beauty of His creation. Say this, "I love you <Your name>. I love you!" Now, find three adjectives that you attach to your person/character and identify three positive things you choose to like and say to yourself. "<Your name>, I like how you _____! You are <adjective>. I admire you."

You are a Gift

Dear heart, you are a gift. You; yes, you; my beautiful sister-daughter-friend-mother are the apple of God's eye. You are His best work. You are God's beloved. Princess/Queen _____ (put your name here) with your shade of mocha, vanilla Swiss almond, dark chocolate, white chocolate, caramel, and all that is in between; you are a gift from and to God and others. Until you accept and believe this you will be a grand piano never tuned and played. Consider this; what if you asked your parent(s) for a specific gift for your birthday or Christmas, you didn't know they were anticipating you coming sooner or later to ask. And they say they don't know if they can get it. Then the following infamous statement comes, "We'll see."

You wait on pins and needles. After asking the first time, you might ask one or two more times. Then it rings out, "Stop asking me... If you keep asking me, you won't get." As a child, you miss that the statement ("you won't get it") was an indicator that either they already had it or they were going to get. After all, what parent who knows how to give good gifts to their children would not give their child that and more (Luke 11:13)?

Now back at waiting on your gift, you are anticipating, Christmas or your birthday morning. It is drawing near! The day arrives and you open your gifts and discover it's there. *Sike!* They got it! How you cherish that gift?! The receiving encompasses the journey of asking, waiting, the buildup, and the opening to receive the long-awaited gift and now your mission is accomplished. The same is true for you and me. You are a gift; a treasure that God took pleasure in creating you and presenting you to the world.

Second Corinthian 7:7 tells us that we have a treasure (Christ in you and me the Hope of Glory) in jars of clay (our bodies) to show that the all-surpassing power (The Holy Spirit) that is from God (because He loves us) and not from us. Now, if our earthly parents know how to give good gifts, how much more will our Father in Heaven give us the Holy Spirit (as a gift) if we ask Him!

Listen, beloved; according to God's Word, there is no good thing withheld from you when you are seeking Him for His will and way. HE desires to bless you. Receiving, accepting, and appreciating His gift of Jesus, His Spirit, His love, His Word, His forgiveness, and Him calling you His own are the best ways to receive His gifts daily. You are God's workmanship created in Him and by Him; in His image and likeness to do good works.

So, I ask you again, who told you, you were that, or not that, or could not be that; whatever *THAT* might be? Way too often, intentionally, and unintentionally, we have had negative words spoken over us, and we have agreed with them. Agreeing to negativism is easy to do when you are not aware of the opposite of the negative.

EXERCISE

Do this: Whoever "they" were or are that said what you could not do or would not be; right now out of your mouth, counterattack those negative words and speak what you desire and what will be. Keep saying it until you feel it deep in your belly – in your soul.

Keep saying it until your mind stops telling you that pessimism is your reality and truth. Tell yourself you are a gift, a human gift filled with gifts and talents, and abilities. As a gift with gifts, you were created, formed, and designed with and for a purpose. His Word says, *"Before I formed you in the womb, I knew you before you were born, I set you apart; ... (Jer. 1:5)."* You are a gift, and someone needs exactly what God has put in you to help others.

You Rock

In Psalm 139, David is speaking directly to God about us and to us about God. In verses 13 through 18, he tells us about how God is all-knowing. His omniscience is celebrated in this passage as David reminds himself and us that God knows everything about everything and everybody that is in the universe, including you. The Scriptures says,

"... Lord, You knitted me together in my mother's womb. I praise you because I am fearfully and

wonderfully made; your works are wonderful; I know that full well. My frame was not hidden from you when I was made in the secret place, when I was woven together in the depths of the earth. Your eyes saw my unformed body; all the days ordained for me were written in your book before one of them came to be. How precious to me are your thoughts, God! How vast is the sum of them! Where I to count them, they would outnumber the grains of sand—when I awake, I am still with you."

Verse 14 tells us that each of us is fearfully and wonderfully made. But what does that mean? Fearfully means marvelously or awesomely made. Just as God allowed your great-grandparents to come together to get your grandparents here, they came together to get your parents here, and your parents came together for the sole purpose of you getting here. Why? Because God has a grand purpose and plan for you and your life. It was for this cause you were created and in His image.

As it is with all things God formed, fashioned, and brought forth, HE said those things were good. But when HE created you; mankind, HE said you were VERY GOOD (Genesis 1:31), and then declared that you are marvelous AND wonderful. Are you willing too, can you accept this truth about you? I'm waiting. Say it aloud, *"When God created me,*

HE said His work in me is VERY GOOD. *I was and I am wonderfully made. I am God's masterpiece."*

Now that you have this knowledge and understanding, and accept this truth concerning you, let's talk about why so many of us, specifically young girls, and women, find it hard to receive and apply this truth.

Before we address that, I hear someone asking what does in His image and likeness mean? It means God created you from and, according to His humanity, His human-like nature, and His kindness. Yes, God has a human nature; it is called Jesus. John 1:1-4, 10-14, says,

> *"In the beginning was the Word, and the Word was with God, and the Word was God. He was with God in the beginning. Through Him all things were made; without Him nothing was made that has been made. In Him was life, and that life was the light of all mankind." "He was in the world, and though the world was made through Him, the world did not recognize Him. He came to that which was his own, but his own did not receive Him. Yet to all who did receive Him, to those who believed in his name, he gave the right to become children of God – children born not of natural descent, nor of human decision or a husband's will, but born of God. The Word became flesh and made his dwelling among us. We have seen his glory, the glory of the one and only Son, who came from the Father, full of grace and truth."*

You are, and we are the formal, visible representation of who God is and what He's, really like. For many, if not most, it is a challenge to believe and accept that an all good and perfect God is our Heavenly loving Father and gives us the right to choose Him as our God. Then His Son (Jesus) of no sin and holy choose to die a torturous death for us to be our Savior. With all that HE knew we would do, HE still chose and welcomes us in as His child, friend, and heir to His Kingdom.

The difficulty in managing this is because of what our eyes, hearts, minds, bodies, and ears have been experience has tainted us. The negativity makes it hard to believe and accept what God says about us. I get it, I hear you, *"Why would a holy, loving, forgiving God create me to look like and be like Him... Why would HE adopt me and call me as His friend with all my struggles, sins, and my crazy way of thinking? Why would HE welcome me into His family and choose me as His own?"* As a young woman, and sometimes in my adult years, I thought many of the same things.

You are the visible and spiritual presentation of God.

It can be hard to believe God said you are not only beautiful, but you were also created wonderfully from His magnificent creative mine in His glorious image and brilliant likeness. God could have made any animal in His image and likeness. HE could have breathed His breath into a dog, cat, horse, hippo, a giraffe, a tree, a rock, but HE chose to put His Spirit-His life in you-in us as flawed humans. It was only when HE purposefully and intentionally created humans on the 6th day that HE says, *"This is very good."* Beloved, God loves you; created and formed you. HE so loved you that HE sent His Jesus in agreement to die for you to live here and in eternity.

Being made, according to Their (God the Father, God the Son, and God the Holy Spirit) likeness is to be made according to His character, nature, and Spirit. You are the visible and spiritual presentation of God. You were made and formed on purpose to be "physically" and morally like God. You were created with the heart of God and the mind of Christ. HE so loved you that HE sent His Son Jesus, who agreed to die for you so you could live here in the earth through Him and in eternity with Him.

We who are immoral, frail in our flesh (body), weak to our appetites, and wavering in our minds will certainly fail God. HE knew this and still said, "I choose you *<your name>*. Then HE gave us a way out. HE promised that if we confess our sin (tell the truth about them and call them what

HE calls them) HE would forgive us. And when we ask Him to help us, HE has promised to help us and come to our aid; rescuing us from our sins, bad decisions, and habits. Believe Him; HE promised and HE is faithful to answer and do it. His answer of forgiveness is eternal and based on His grace and mercy. This grace, His grace covers and does not condemn. It forgives, cleanses, and helps us because HE knows we are weak (1 John 1:1, Romans 8:26,27) and struggle to believe and obey. That's the Love of the One and Only Father God in Heaven who created you to look and be like Him. Genesis 1:26-31 tells us that,

> *"Then God said, "Let Us (Father, Son, Holy Spirit) make man in Our image, according to Our likeness [not physical, but a spiritual personality and moral likeness – Our character (which is the Fruit of the Spirit]; and let them have complete authority over the fish of the sea, the birds of the air, the cattle, and over the entire earth, and over everything that creeps and crawls on the earth." So, God created man in His own image, in the image and likeness of God He created him; male and female He created them. And God blessed them [granting them certain authority] and said to them, "Be fruitful, multiply, and fill the earth, and subjugate it [putting it under your power]; and rule over (dominate) the fish of the sea, the birds of the air, and every living thing that moves upon the earth." So God said, "Behold, I have given*

you every plant yielding seed that is on the surface of the entire earth, and every tree which has fruit yielding seed; it shall be food for you; and to all the animals on the earth and to every bird of the air and to everything that moves on the ground—to everything in which there is the breath of life—I have given every green plant for food"; and it was so [because He commanded it]. God saw everything that He had made, and behold, it was very good, and He validated it completely.

Sure, I heard His love for Christians spoken from the pulpit. Yes, Genesis 1 was preached. I heard it said that we were made in His image, but not me specifically. I received compliments here and there, but the concept of being made in His image and likeness was never imparted or instilled in me for greatness. I did not receive it at church, at home, at school or anywhere in my community. Today, my joy is in choosing this truth about God and myself! Hear me beloved, where there is truth and understanding; hope and freedom to *be* what God created (very good, awesome, wonderful, unique, the apple of His eye, His masterpiece, and the list goes on) you to be becomes real, accessible, obtainable, and doable. Listen, all I need is Word!!!

God is great and HE as your creator and you are His child and a Believer in Jesus, HE is in you! I invite you to accept the Great One and be great! Not to be conceded, arrogant or vain, but what God made you to be; like them, in Their image and likeness. I wonder what battles and bad choices I could have avoided had I known who and whose I was as a child, young girl, and a young woman. Again, I stop and restate:

> **NOTE:** *It is crucial and of vital importance that you speak positive affirming and confirming words to your sons and, without a doubt, to your daughters. Sure, moms can do this, but a daddy building his daughter is critical. Because if you don't do it, some other males who may not mean her any good will do it for you!*

My not knowing and accepting this, along with other interruptions that hit my life as a young girl, created all kinds of false truths, substandard behaviors, and habits. Sex as a teen, disobedience to parents, sneaking, risky behavior, and subpar relationships was norm at an early age. Accepting the wrong types of men in my life, dating the drug dealer in college, in my early 20's a married man (didn't know he was married but it still happened), and alike were patterns birth out of a stolen and unenforced identity.

Recommitting my life to Christ at 30 and coming into this knowledge and truth and feeding my soul daily until I believed who God said I was and am caused a transformation in my mind and heart. With a list of wrongs and lies swirling in my head, this took years.

Today I joyfully continue to evolve and I am commitment to being and doing all God created me in His image and likeness to be! Sometimes changing your mind about something that is deeply engrained is not enough. You must allow God to change your heart about it so you can come out of agreement with it. And when you do this, you will change not only what you think, but also how you respond to it and live out who you are.

God formed you to be like Him. HE desires to be with and HE is for you beloved. If you have not, I invite you to choose God the Father as your Heavenly Father God and His Son Jesus as your Savior and Lord. All it takes is you saying,

"Forgive me LORD for my sins. God, I believe You sent Your Son Jesus to die for my sins. I believe that Jesus lived, died for my sins, was buried, and rose. I believe that Jesus is coming back for those who believe. I believe that Jesus is in Heaven. Thank You Jesus for praying for and defending me. I receive You as my Savior and Lord. Thank You for leaving me the

Your Holy Spirit. Move into and live in my heart; lead and guide me."

If you confessed this, you are saved. You are not only God's creation, you are now His child and apart of the family of God. God is your all-powerful, all-knowing, all-wise God and loving Heavenly Father. You are an heir of God and a joint-heir with Christ. You are His friend, His prize, and the apple of His eye. You are in The Will of God. Jesus is not only your Savior and Lord; HE is your big brother, intercessor and defense attorney in Heaven. The Holy Spirit is your help and comforter. With Them, you can do all things, and you will do great things. You are unstoppable. Seek Him; receive Him as your Father-God-Savior and Lord. Then talk to and with Him, tell Him, ask Him, watch Him, and learn Him. It may not always be when or how you want Him be His answer will be exactly what you need at that time in that season.

I invite and encourage you to love you and like you. You might as well sweetie because HE does. Always remember, you are the image of God. You are fearfully, wonderfully, and beautifully made! You are loved. You are amazing. You were and are worth it. You ROCK!

A Message to My Younger Me

Dear Younger Me,

Hey you. I need to tell you that you rock. You are amazing. I wish you could have peeked into your future and saw who you would become and yet are becoming and what you would do. You didn't know you would be suited to bear the image of God: to be His voice, a reason and wisdom too so many. You didn't know His creation of you was on point and for purpose. You were and are His beautiful creation. The beautiful image of Him in you started as an inside job. What you saw and experienced caused you to struggle; to think you were ugly, that your nose was too wide, your lips too big, and chubbiness was unacceptable. Yet, HE called it all wonderful. Did you know that is one of the names God called Jesus, "A wonderful counselor?" And look at you, today, a wonderful, wise counselor, encourager, and mentor too many: girls, boys, and adult men and women! You were so much fun and happy before that happen; before you heard and experienced hurtful words and actions at school and by your father toward your mom and siblings. I must be honest, sometimes I can't remember our childhood and times of joy, peace, and laughter, but I do remember you were happy. I am proud of you. To see and know that you have forgiven him and have used your healing to help transform the lives of other young ladies and women and how you are such a powerful witness that forgiveness is possible. Forgive me for not checking in with you more to make sure you were ok on the inside and encouraging you to talk to other adults that you trusted. Your words, transparency and vulnerability are a healing agent to help others heal their heart and father relationship. I know it took a while for the inside created image of God to align with the reflection of His likeness, but you did it. You made it. Those that encounter you see it and they experience God because you did the work to be healed and to participate in your victory and wholeness journey. Recognizing and accepting that you are a one-of-a-kind, beautiful, physical, and spiritual image of God has been amazing to watch. I, along with others are often awe-stroke by your love for and submission to Him. Oh, Tuesday, if only you could have known then how very much God loved and loves you and would use you to reach millions. If only you would have known how deserving you are to accept your greatness. Just think of all that you imaged sitting on that table in front of your bedroom window on Pipestone. And now you are pursuing it to be and have it all. Better now than never. You had a slow start, but your finish is strong! You are a strong, power woman of God, loyal friend and amazing daughter and person. You surrendered to God and fo'real this time; gave him the script of your life that HE had already written. You gave Him total permission to direct and navigate your story and your life. And when I say your future is bright - that is an understatement. Your best is truly yet to come. Eyes have not seen and ears have not heard the things-the things God has in store for you simply because you love Him. Remember how you used to get in trouble for talking in class and *helping others do their work? Well, that is what you are doing now! Even then you were a voice for others and used your gift of speaking and teaching to encourage and help others. You and I know that sometimes you helped people do and get their work done because you just wanted someone to talk too and play with, but we will keep that as our secret. Even then, you were always a loyal friend. Guess what, you still are, and I admire that about you. Remember when mama ironed and laid your clothes out for school and how well dressed you were. Well today, you still bring it! Now that shoe game is something to be both revered and rejected - girl you got too many. LOL. I'm sorry for the things said to you that hurt and damaged your soul and your opinion of yourself. Today, I would be your defender. I would interrupt those words that became thoughts (strongholds) and manifested in uncharacteristic behaviors. I would not let anyone say or do anything to you that could damage or hurt you inside or outside. You have been through and weather a lot, but you made it. Yet, because of it you are who you are today. Your faith and walk with God is* something to be admired. Actually, it is. Who would have known? We thought it was law school but God had another law in mind; His Word. You are a wise, integral, purposeful, powerful, exceptional woman of God. Yes, of God!!! HE uses you in supernatural ways. Too many, you are an example and a mentor. I hope you are proud of me: the woman I have become in your name and God's. I love you, girlie. There is so much more I could say to you and the girls and young women who are reading this, but I will end here. Please know that you – all of you are fearfully and wonderfully made, exceptionally bearing the image and likeness of God. Remember, everyone is an image-bearer: bearing the glorious image of God. Respect yourself and other image bearers. Love and serve God. Place Him first and make lover of you soul. HE has a perfect plan for your life, ask Him, and HE will tell and guide you in it!

Beautifully made in the Image of God,
Lovingly Tuesday

Jewlya Payne

Jewlya is a wife, a mother, a college graduate, and a woman who loves God. Jewlya attended Indiana University Purdue University - Indianapolis where she obtained a bachelor's degree in Criminal Justice. She has been married for 3 years to her wonderful husband Nathan and has a beautiful 9-month-old baby girl named Rhylee. Jewlya is employed with the Marion County Probation Department as an Adult Probation Officer and has been for the last two years. Jewlya loves to read and write and would always write short stories as a teenager. She helped write and direct a church play at the age of 15. Jewlya attends the Streams Church and serves as a Care Coach and an Intercessor. She finds fulfillment and purpose in helping and encouraging others.

Are You The One?
~by Jewlya Payne~

He sent them to the Lord to ask, *"Are you the one who is to come, or should we expect someone else?* (Luke 7:19. NIV)" Throughout my life, I have always asked this question as it related to my relationships. As a young girl, I grew up thinking and dreaming about my wedding day. Playing dress up and pretending to walk down the aisle, marrying my dolls off, and constantly asking my mother to see her wedding pictures. I grew up in a two-parent household, and my parents were married, so married couples were my norm.

As I got older, my desire for relationship and one day marriage grew strong. I wanted a boyfriend. I remember the first time I told my parents about a boy that I liked. I was about 13 years old. He was my pastor's son, and I was his sister's best friend. I remember the crush I had on him. I asked his sister to exchange a note for me that expressed my interest in him. I thought to myself, "I have found the one." Pretty young to be thinking that, right? I recalled the first time we had a conversation. We had absolutely nothing in common. Young love. He told me that once he was old enough, he would no longer serve God because of all the pressure of being a pastor's kid. Even at the age of 13, I knew that was a red flag. I grew up in a household where God was the foundation, and anything aside from Him was wrong.

I enjoyed growing up in church, going to Vacation Bible School, singing in the choir, and acting in the skits and plays we often had. I accepted Jesus as my Lord and Savior and got baptized at the age of 12, but I was in my 20s when I understood what it truly meant to live for Jesus. At school, I was 'the good' girl who was always at church. I was not allowed to spend the night at friends' houses unless my parents knew all their information: addresses, phone numbers, people who were there, and I had better be where I said I was going to be. I had a strict curfew. I was not allowed to go to parties, and if friends came over, my parents' rules applied to them as well.

My father was a deacon, and my mother was my Sunday School teacher. What choice did I have? I remember we had a picture that said, "As for me and my house, we will serve the Lord." And man did my parents make sure of it. To me, serving the Lord meant going to church when I was supposed to, being an upright person, and what my parents stressed to me often, obeying them. They even had scripture to back this claim. Ephesians 6:3 NLT says, *"If you honor your father and mother, things will go well for you, and you will have a long life on the earth."* Who didn't want to live a long life?

Chasing Ishmaels

Have you ever heard the story of Abraham and his sons Isaac and Ishmael? In the bible, Abraham and his wife Sarah had been trying to conceive a child. Sarah was old and was barren, which means incapable of producing offspring (children). Sarai had a handmaid by the name of Hagar, and out of impatience, Sarai suggested that Abraham take Hagar and produce a child.

Now, I forgot to mention that God had already promised Abraham that he would have an heir. Hagar conceived and bore a son that she named Ishmael. Sarah despised Hagar and mistreated her, so Hagar fled. These events are in the book of Genesis chapters 16-21. I bring up this story because I have encounters with some Ishmaels, and I allowed them in my life knowing God had already promised me an Isaac.

In high school, there was a rule to being popular: participate in sports and date the cutest guy in school. I did not always date the cutest guy, but I felt the need to have a boyfriend - ALL the time. My first boyfriend was a boy who was in the marching band. He wasn't the most handsome guy, but he was cute to me. In high school, I sang in the gospel choir. The band room and the choir room were next to each other except for a door dividing the rooms. One day after exiting the choir room, I saw him. He was about 6-feet tall, brown-skinned, had braids, and was a year ahead of me.

He wore clothes that were too big for him, but that was the style in the mid-2000s. He walked past me and smiled, and I smiled back. I had a friend who was in the band, and I expressed my interest in him. About two weeks later, I joined band class. Why? Because of him, of course. I played the clarinet for a little while in middle school, and I was not very good at it, but that was my way in, my ticket. I went to my guidance counselor and was placed in band class the next day.

He played the trombone and sat in the second row. I sat in the front and was often getting lectured for playing the wrong note. Even now, I laugh at the fact that I went through all of that for a boy. Later in life I learned that I should never chase the guy. I remember the first day I walked into the band room; it felt like everyone was staring at me. I knew a couple of people, and they asked why I had transferred out of the choir. I advised that I had played the clarinet in middle school and missed playing.

Now, I knew good-and-well that was not the reason, but I refused to appear that I was thirsty to get to know him, even though I was. I remember one day in the band room while being lectured for playing the wrong note, as usual, and he took up for me. The band teacher was grilling me, and he said something; then, the teacher kicked him out of the class for getting smart. I caught up to him later in the day and thanked him; he smiled and went on his way.

I got butterflies: it was something about his silence that was interesting and intriguing. We were preparing for a basketball game and I had to learn the "boogie drill," a dance that the band performed to get the crowd hype. He was assigned to teach me the dance. FINALLY... A moment alone. I had no rhythm, and we stayed after school all evening until I became acquainted with the moves. He was even quieter, then. It took for me to ask questions for him to start talking. Although there was another young man, a cute senior, who had been trying to get my attention, I was not as interested.

The week before Memorial Day weekend, we stayed after school for a basketball game. After the game, I was on my way to my locker, and I cut through the cafeteria. He came up behind me and picked me up, and we started play fighting. He attempted to throw me in the trashcan, but was unsuccessful. When we got to my locker, he asked me to be his girlfriend. We became a couple and I thought that he was going to be the man I married. I was serious about our relationship and no one could tell me nothing. I was 16-years old and in love; well, at least I thought I was. We were inseparable.

We stayed up all night on the phone, visited each other, and stayed after school with one another. It was the summer before my junior year of high school, and I was a virgin. The sex talk with my parents was nothing intense or formal. My mom's take on it was "just don't do it." My dad's take on it was "you're like an apple on a tree that is not ripe enough, don't let some boy pick you off before it is your time."

I was 16 and my hormones and feelings were raging, but I did not want to be known as "that girl." You know that girl that all the other girl's gossip about, and the one that all the guys call easy-to-get. At the time, my boyfriend wanted to take the next step in our relationship to sex, but I was unsure. He would let up for a while but sooner or later, we would be discussing the topic again.

I remember one summer day I was at a friend's house, and he texts me to ask if I wanted to come over and hang out. He lived a couple of blocks over, and we decided to meet half way. We got to his house, and for a moment I felt that I should not be there, but I stayed. We walked in and it was quiet. He told me that his mom was going to be gone for a couple of hours and that we could hang out in his bedroom. We started watching a movie and as the saying goes, one thing led to another.

At first, I hesitated, but then he said, "I love you." Those words meant everything to me; they made me feel accepted. I lost my virginity that day. I pictured my first time to be like the scene in the movie Love and Basketball. You know, music in the background, sensual and all that stuff. Movies sure do have a way of getting your hopes up. This encounter had no music, no fireworks, no excitement. It was nothing to write home about.

When his mother came home, she offered to drive me back to my friend's house. I left full of disappointment and regret. Something I had held on to and cherished was gone that fast, and I could not get it back. I remember thinking I should have waited until marriage. I cried because I felt that I was not special anymore and that my value had been stripped away from me. I never told my mom until years later. I was afraid of disappointing her, and we did not discuss these kinds of things.

We continued to date and have sex. I cared about him, and I wanted a boyfriend. I thought that if we did not have sex, he would break up with me, and I did not want to be alone. Also, I felt connected to him, and that caused me to continue to give up the goods. It had become a "soul tie." They are real and can disrupt your life, but I will discuss that a little later in the chapter.

He came back to school a senior, and I came back to school a junior and a woman, at least I thought. The school year passed, he graduated, and we went our separate ways. It was rough. We tried to stay in touch, but the phone calls and his visits home became less and less. It was my high school senior year, and there I met him - another him - whom I thought I would marry and be with for the rest of my life. You would've thought that I learned my lesson with the first one. I hadn't had sex since the first one left and went to college, and I found myself often thinking about it but never acting on it. My motto was, don't have sex unless he's a boyfriend, not unless you are married. Boy, how that had changed.

He was a junior, and his sister and I were seniors and had a couple of classes together. I transferred back to the choir my senior year. I remember seeing him walk into the room for his piano class while I was leaving, and we made eye contact. He was officially on my mind. I asked my sister about him because people who played basketball knew each other. She told me that it was Showtime's brother. I told her that I thought he was cute; she laughed. She told me that I had interesting taste in guys. He was different, but he was fine, to me. Someone must have told him I liked him because I started seeing him more than usual in the hallways.

Eventually, he asked someone to get my phone number, and the relationship started. Sometimes we would skip class or stay after school together. I was running track, found myself ditching track practice to hang out with him at his house. When I did attend track practice, I was not focused. My coach often addressed my tardiness and missing practice, but I did not care because I was in a new relationship and was crushing hard. As we continued to date, it became prevalent that he and his father did not have a healthy relationship. I tried my best to be there for him: making myself available in so many ways became draining. He would leave home and walk to my house, which was far.

We would sit on my porch and discuss what he went through at home and how he couldn't wait to move out. We eventually became sexually active and would sneak around to do it. I would tell my dad that I was going to stay after school for homework, track practice, or some function, but I would to his house instead. I felt terrible for sneaking around and lying to my parents, but a part of me enjoyed the thrill. Oh, the struggle of being the "good girl."

I even got bold enough to sneak him in when my parents were home. He had got dropped off one evening, and I remember sneaking him in through my bedroom window. I turned the shower on to muffle the noise and locked my bedroom door. I woke up that morning to a knock on my door from my mother asking me to unlock my door. I quickly told him to hide on the side of my bed, and we waited patiently for my parents to leave for the day. I must have been feeling bold because that is something I would have never done on my own accord. That day, we had our first argument.

He had been on his phone and was making sure to hold it to where I was unable to see it. He sat his phone on my bed and went to the bathroom. I was curious, so I decided to look through his messages. He had been texting another girl as if he did not have a girlfriend. We ended up having a break-up-to-make-up relationship. How many times I took him back...? Too many to count. Senior year came to an end, and we still decided to date when I went to college. I wish someone had told me not to enter college while in a relationship.

Freshman year was stressful. I had 18-credit hours, worked at McDonald's full-time, and had a boyfriend in high school who decided to stop trusting me. He would accuse me of cheating on him, and later I would find out why. He would often call me while he was in class, and those phone calls would end in arguments. I started sending him money so he could visit me, and I would also go home to see him - often. Eventually, I began to look at other guys because our relationship was very unhealthy, and I was tired of exerting my energy and exhausting my funds to keep a wounded relationship afloat.

There were some fine men in college. Some were trying to get at your girl, but I was committed to my relationship. Well, at least that's what I was telling people and myself. But to be completely honest, I was no longer feeling it or him. I felt like I was missing out on college life. So, I decided to start partying. I hung out with a group of three girls who I had met in my dorm. We were all in relationships and going through it. We decided that our boyfriends weren't worth the stress, and we began to party, going to fraternity houses, and drinking.

One night we went to the Alpha House for a party kickback. As I was entering, my boyfriend called. He asked what I was doing, and before I knew it, we were arguing - again! He told me I had changed, and he missed when I was innocent and just focused on him. One of my girls saw me looking upset; so, she snatched my phone, hung up, and put my phone in her purse. When we walked, we went straight to where they were making drinks. Honestly, I don't remember how much I had to drink, but I know I was intoxicated. We danced and laughed all night. I remember stumbling to the door to go outside because it was hot inside.

Some guy helped me out the door and asked if we could talk. Not even five minutes into the conversation, I began to cry. I was sobbing, and he just stared at me. I told him how I come from a Christian family and that my parents would be upset with me if they knew what I was doing. I ranted on about my upbringing and how I knew better. I was feeling, no, convicted, by the Holy Spirit. But, beyond my liquor-induced tears, I ignored it. I continued to party, drink, and even started smoking marijuana; well, I tried it.

The next day, I had a hangover but tried to make it to class. I was still in that relationship, and we were still having our ups and downs. I started to struggle in my studies and eventually quit my job because it became too much. By the end of the first semester, I was on academic probation. I needed to focus and reevaluate why I was there. My major was Criminology, and I had the dream of being a lawyer. I had wanted to be a lawyer since I was 8-years old. My grades and life had me rethinking what I wanted to do and doubting myself.

Near the end of the school year, and one of the girls that I hung out with had gotten into it with me, and we were no longer on speaking terms. She had spread lies and rumors about me to the other girls. The fall out between us had gotten out of hand to the point that she started threatening to beat me up. Now let's be clear, I've never been a punk, but wouldn't fight unless it was necessary. I didn't care about all the talking she was doing as long as she didn't step to me or touch me. She was bold when her friends were around but would never say a word when she was alone. And, oh yeah, she even contacted my boyfriend and told him that I had cheated on him.

During the week of finals, my stress was at an all-time high. It had been rough trying to balance a part-time job, 18-credit hours, and a rocky relationship. So, here I was in the dorm lounge area studying, and the girl walked in. All I could think was, if this girl even looks my way, it's going down.

She smirked and talked to some other girls that were in the area. I held my tongue, but something felt off. Before I knew it, someone threw a balled-up piece of paper at me. I stood up and advised her that she better be lucky that she had missed. She walked over to me and got in my face.

When I told her to move, she punched me in the face. I must have blacked out because all I remember is some girls screaming and pulling me off her. I got called into my RA's room, and they told me that I was not allowed on the floor anymore even though she had started the whole thing. In the last two weeks of school, I had to move from the 10th floor to the 3rd floor of the building. At least I did not have to run up and down all those stairs if the elevator broke.

Freshman year ended, and I was ready to go home for the summer. I was drained and needed the break. At the time, my on-and-off boyfriend had graduated high school and was on his way to Indiana State University in the Fall. I felt relief because now we could go to the same school and spend time with one another. Boy, was I wrong!

We continued to date, but he would question me about the people I hung out with on campus and reminded me that he had not forgotten that the girl who told him I had cheated on him. We had fights and arguments, and things got worse between us. We began to see less and less of one another, and he started making excuses as to why we could not hang out.

I hung out with a different crowd during my sophomore year and began to smoke marijuana more frequently. One day, I went to the cafeteria to grab food, and I saw my boyfriend with another girl. He claimed that she was just a friend and that there was nothing to worry about, but I did not believe him. I recall a time when we were supposed to go to the library, and I could not reach him. Instead, I showed up at his dorm, and the roommate was there.

He told me that he had not been staying there because some girl was there all the time. I decided to stay and wait for him to come to his room. Once his roommate left, I began snooping. Not to my surprise, I found the girl's clothes in his dresser and picture of them. It seemed to have been a picture from one of those photo booths in the mall. It was her! The girl he told me not to worry about because they were just "friends."

I lost it! I trashed his room! Ripped up the picture, took clothes out of the dresser and threw them on the floor; I took the sheets, comforter, and mattress off the bed and threw it on the floor, and sat on his bed crying. We met up, and he told me he was done with me and had moved on.

Isn't that crazy how we do that as females. All for the sake of saying we have a boyfriend or a man, we would rather subject ourselves to misery than not have a "man."

I had devoted a lot of time and energy to the relationship. Our toxicity had become the norm for me. What was I going to do without him? You would have thought that I would have focused on my studies and got my stuff together, but no, I was checking his social media and asking people about him. I found out through a mutual friend that he had moved off-campus.

And to put the icing on the cake, the girl was pregnant. I became depressed. I stopped going to my classes, smoked, and partied more. When the semester was over, I decided I was not coming back. I went home and started working at McDonald's.

Danger Ahead

So here I was, a college dropout working at McDonald's and living back at home with my parents. My co-workers notified me that my ex-boyfriend had been coming to my job with his pregnant girlfriend. Luckily, I was never there. I don't know what I would have done. I was trying to get my life together and figure out what my next move was. I decided to apply to Texas Southern University. I needed to get away and start on a clean slate. I asked my sister to go with me, and we started the process of looking for apartments. I was excited because my favorite uncle lived there.

Unfortunately, my sister bailed on me at the last minute. I did not want to go or be there without her. I continued to work and decided to enroll in some courses at Ivy Tech. While there, it happens again. I met him. Yea, you know the phrase by now - the man I thought I would marry. I was broken and desperate. Honestly, I wasn't over my ex-boyfriend.

A close friend of mine, who happened to be my boss, had met a guy. He came to see her at work, and he brought his friend. He said little and seemed to be shy. After I had got off work, we sat out in my friend's car talking. He asked for my phone number, and we began having regular conversations. We set a date to go out. My friend had agreed to do my hair, and her guy friend and his friend showed up.

I was embarrassed because I was sitting on the floor with my hair looking a mess, and she had not started braiding it yet. He came over to where I was and smiled excessively big. I told him to get out of my face because I looked a mess. He laughed and told me I looked beautiful. That was it! We began to spend more time together.

Consistently, without missing a beat, he would wait for me in the parking lot to get off work. I was enjoying his company, but I didn't want to rush into another relationship. He was persistent, and I was lonely. He came to my job one evening and asked me to be his girlfriend. A part of me was hesitant, but I said yes, and we began dating.

Like most new relationships, we were spending a lot of time together, and we were in love. I was taking classes at Ivy Tech, and he was a lifeguard at Douglas Park. Things were smooth sailing in the beginning. He was kind, affectionate, and made sure he took care of me. But somewhere, things took an ugly turn. The relationship became abusive. I'll never forget the day I was at my mother's house, disarrayed with cuts on my face and glass in my hair, and the police were at my front door taking my statement.

He left with a warning to get out now or end up dead. He had many issues and would often use marijuana to cope or suppress. I introduced him to my family, and he would even attend church with me most Sundays. I remember meeting his family for the first time.

Usually, parents loved me, but that was not the case with his parents. I met his grandmother, first, who appeared to be intoxicated. She called me names and told me that her grandson was bipolar, but that he was a good man. Why that did not raise a red flag, I don't know? There were so many signs, and numerous times I should have ended it and left, but I ignored them to be in a relationship. We became sexually involved, and sex blinded me.

Earlier I mentioned soul ties. According to an article I read on "proverbs2426.com," it noted that the most commonly known soul tie definition is that "soul ties are spiritual connections formed through a sexual relationship." I became extremely attached to him. I ignored all the things that in, a non-sexual relationship, I would have run and not look back. I would often feel mentally, physically, and emotionally drained after being around him. He could be so negative and unsupportive. He would get attitudes with me and then apologize, only to do it again.

Our first fight happened about 6 or 7 months into the relationship. After the first came others. Not to trivialize it, but we fought plenty of times, and many times it got physical. The signs of him being abusive were there, but I ignored them. I placed them in individual boxes or incidents. Standing-alone, they didn't look like a problem, but collectively he was what his grandmother said, bipolar. Hoping he would change and stop, I subjected myself to experience the pain of an angry, abusive person.

Were there signs or red flags? Yes. His demeanor would change quickly with me and around my friends and family, and he was very argumentative and would pick fights for the sake of arguing and fighting. He would blow-up and apologize only to do it again - it was a vicious cycle; he was jealous of me, my desire for school and better, my friends, and my family; and, he was possessive of me and my time.

The fight: I was at his house, and we had spent most of the day together. It had been a long day, and I had a class in the morning. He told me that he thought it was stupid for me to leave and that I should stay with him. I told him no and made my way to the door. He stood in front of the door and asked me where I was going. I told him home. His roommate was in the living room and was telling him to let me leave. He began to call me names and said that he didn't trust me. I told him that I didn't have time for his mess (I probably used another word, but that was then).

Before I knew it, he was pulling me by my hair and had thrown me on the couch and was in my face yelling. I was heated! I kicked him in between the legs, which caused him to buckle, and I was able to get to the door and leave. I drove home crying and very upset, but I didn't tell anyone. He called apologizing and telling me that it would never happen again.

Our second fight was worse than the first. Once again, we got into it because I needed to get home and study for an exam. We argued about me leaving, and before I knew it, I was being called names and accused me of cheating. I walked outside and got in my car. He was beating on the window, telling me to unlock my doors. I did not feel safe. I felt a feeling that I needed to leave and fast. I tried to start my car, and it stalled. Before I knew it, glass had shattered all over my face.

He had picked up a slab of concrete and busted my window with it. He unlocked the door and pushed me out of the driver's seat into the passenger's seat. I looked down, and there was blood on my pants. I couldn't process what had just happened. He started the car, sped off down the street, yelling and cussing at me. I asked him to let me out of the car, but he told me he was taking me home.

I was shook-and-shocked! I had never been in this type of situation before. Once again, I asked him to stop the car and let me out. He told me to shut up and advised that if I asked again, he was going to wreck the car with us in it. I sat back, cried, and prayed to God that I would make it home safely.

We pulled up to my house, and I got out and ran to the door. My mother opened the door, and she was bout ready to kill him. My mom asked me what happened, and I gave her the rundown. My mother told him to leave, and he refused. She pulled me inside and called the police. By the time the police came, he had left. My mother was furious! The officer spoke with me and asked what had happened. He looked at me and advised me to get out of the relationship before it was too late.

I was exhausted trying to help and love someone who hurt me...

After the officer left, I went to the bathroom to take a good look at myself. I sobbed as I observed the cuts on my face and fragments of glass in my hair. I looked intensely at the woman in the mirror. I did not recognize her. When had she (I) become so naïve and a pushover? I had allowed all this for a toxic man and an unhealthy relationship! My mother came in and consoled me.

She sat me down, and we had a talk about my decisions and that I needed to leave him alone. A few days passed, and he ended up messaging me on Facebook. I ignored him for about a week, but he was persistent. I gave in, and we began sneaking around to see one another. Now you may be asking, "Why is this girl still messing with this man?" I asked myself that same question!

I never uncovered the answer. I assumed I was obsessed with trying to fix flawed men; I mean boys. Maybe I was trying to mold them into the person I wanted them to be. I was exhausted trying to help and love someone who hurt me and didn't want to be helped or loved. It tore me apart. I was physically, mentally, and emotionally broken. It was a vicious cycle, and for some reason, it felt like the norm to me. Then it got worse.

Jewlya to the Rescue

He and his parents were at odds with one another; so, they kicked him out, and he went to stay with his grandmother. One day she would want him there, and the next day she was threatening to kick him out, too. It got so bad that he ended up staying at a homeless shelter for two weeks. By now, I had left school again (Ivy Tech) and started working downtown as a server at the One America Square building.

We were still secretly seeing one another. I was allowing him to use my car while I was at work, and he would pick me up at the end of my shift. Way too often, he would be, and this would provoke arguments. I broke up with him and was done with him and the relationship for good. My sister found out that we were dating again. She very upset and told me that I had better not go back to him.

I had gone to a birthday party with my sister. Due to having too much to drink, we decided to stay the night there. I was sad about not being with him, but I knew it was for the best. I remember getting a phone call early in the morning from him. I woke up and crept out of the room so that no one could hear me. He told me that a friend was supposed to take him to work but had bailed on him. He sounded desperate as he sought to convince me to take him to work. I sensed that something was not right. I know now that was Holy Spirit.

But I ignored it and went back into the room to get my belongings. I sent him a text message notifying him that I would be at his house within 30-minutes. I must have been making a lot of noise because my sister woke up. I lied to her saying, I was going to take a girlfriend of mine to work. She told me that I had better not be lying and be on my way to see him. I assured her that I wasn't and left.

As I drove, I experienced anxiety; an intense uncertainty overwhelmed me. I felt a pit sink into my stomach and thought to pull over, but I did not. When I arrived, I called and let him know that I was outside. As usual, his demeanor was off; he seemed to always be in a funk. But this time, I assumed it was because he was running late for work. I unlocked the door, and he got in. He looked at me and asked how I had been doing. I told him that I was fine. He buckled his seatbelt and gave me a strange look. He sat back and asked why the seat was adjusted so far back, and then without me being able to answer, the accusations came spewing out of his mouth.

He accused me of having another man in the car. I told him that I had gone to a birthday party the night before and that one of my girls must have adjusted the seat. He called me a liar. I told him to get out of my car. He apologized and asked me to take him to work. We were driving down 38th street (a very busy street in the city), and I began to play the Jeezy CD that was in my car.

He looked at me and asked what man had given me the CD. I told him that my girl had left it in my car the night before. Once again, he called me a liar. We were at the stoplight. The light was red. I again asked him to get out of my car. He told me to keep driving.

For a brief moment, I hesitated. I wanted to act strong and not afraid. But as the light turned green, I continued to drive. Suddenly, he changed the gear to park, and I put it back into drive and pulled over into a parking lot. We began to argue and fight. Yes, fight. I tried to get out of the car, but he pulled me back in and punched me in my side. He uttered the words "B****, I'll kill you!" And at that moment, I truly believed every word and fear set in. I cried and fought until I was able to get out of the car. I ran to a barbershop and banged on the door, praying that someone would answer.

A woman unlocked the door, let me in, and locked it behind us. She asked me what was going on, and before I knew it, he was outside the door screaming for me to come outside. I told her that he was my ex-boyfriend and we had got into a fight and he was trying to hurt me. As she asked him to leave, she got on the phone and dialed 911. He continued to shout and told her that he was not going to leave until she released me.

The woman stated that she was not releasing me and that the police were on the way. He picked up a slab of concrete and threw it at the window, breaking the first barrier of glass and then took off on foot. As I sobbed, she tried to console me. She told me that God must be looking out for me because no one is ever there at that time and that she was there only because she came back to get her wallet.

The police showed up, my parents and sister as well, and I gave a statement. I walked outside to see that he had busted out four car windows, and the side door dented. My mother was angry - bloody angry - and my sister looked at me with disappointment. I rode home in silence as they yelled at me; I had spaced out. I was traumatized; broken; had hit rock bottom. I felt that there was no way I could pick up these pieces and live again.

Where was my dad during all this? Well, like a lot of dads, he was active at the beginning of my relationship: talking with me, to me, about boys. Like most dads, though, he did not like any of my boyfriends. Well, except for Nathan and even that took a minute. During this last abusive relationship, he was going through some things of his own and was not present that much. Would that have helped...? Maybe. But, ultimately, my being with him and staying with him was my choice: an unhealthy and almost life-altering one. Surely, God was with me.

He uttered the words, "B****, I'll kill you!"

The Switch

He ended up going to jail, and I filed a restraining order against him. I was summoned to court and decided not to press charges. Why...? I just wanted to move on with my life and get to a place of normalcy - whatever that was. After that one-year toxic relationship, I switched. I went back to school and started to focus on me to change for the betterment of my future. I began to have dreams, and God began to speak to me during this new season of my life. I recommitted my life to Him and asked God to send godly people into my life, and He did. I started going back to church, conferences, and building a personal relationship with Jesus.

Through this, my heart and soul began to mend. I joined the church, and the power of God filled me. We call this baptized in the Holy Spirit. I was learning and growing in the things of God. I no longer desired to drink, smoke, or have sex without a ring. Don't get me wrong; I struggled! But God was my Keeper. I messed up on many occasions, but I continued to seek God for wholeness. His love, grace, and forgiveness became real. The more I grew in the knowledge of God, the closer I was drawn to Him. I dared not to test His grace and forgiveness; I respected His saving love that had spared my life. I was so busy enjoying my relationship with the Lord and my season of singleness that I did not notice him. Yes, him; the him who was the one!

This time I knew better. My thoughts were no longer about is this the one I would marry or if I would spend the rest of my life with him. He was just him. He had commented on a Facebook picture of mine, and friendship kindled. I was not trying to have a boyfriend but a friendship. He pursued me, but I kept my guard up.

I prayed and prayed about this young man: something I can't recall if I had done with the others. All I felt radiating from him was peace and safety. What was it about him that made this experience different? As I considered this, his qualities were quite the opposite of the red flags I had received from other guys and the abuser.

Come to find out, we had attended the same college and he liked me back then but knew I had a boyfriend. Now, five years later, here we were. We were enjoying each other's time, conversation, and company. We began dating, and he began attending my church and he got involved in ministry. Things were moving fast, but God was in it. If I spent time giving every detail, we would have another book, so I'll give you a quick timeline and fast-forward.

We met in August 2015, began dating in November 2015. got engaged in October 2016 and got married in July 2017. In May 2018, I graduated with a bachelor's degree, and we had our daughter in August of 2019. Wow, right? God has blessed me with my Isaac. All before him were experiences, experiments, and Ishmaels. Were things perfect in our dating and courtship? No. Were we always on the same page? No. At times are things difficult? Yes. Of course, it would be. God did not promise perfection.

We are individuals with our personalities and behaviors that God says shall become one. Shall become is a process. I am grateful that God let a man find me and gave me someone who seeks God on our behalf. If someone were to ask me if I knew God had all of this for me, I would have said no, and I would not have believed God or anyone. The past, the pain, hurt, abuse, and brokenness are just that - a thing of my past.

Qualities that set a man apart

- Feel safe; very respectful
- Spends time with your parents
- Always makes sure you get home safely
- Always checked on you
- Prays with you and for you
- Helped you with school/job work
- Opens your door, *which I got upset about because I wasn't used to it*
- Asks you about your visions and dreams and how he could help you achieve them
- Calm and gentle
- Great listener

A Message to My Younger Me

Dear Younger Me,

If only you knew what you could achieve and be. If only you knew the light and gifts that God placed on the inside of you. God had already paid the ultimate price for you before any man ever tried to determine your value. You are already beautiful, and you do not need the validation or confirmation from a man. You do not need relationships with a man or to have sex with them to feel loved and wanted. God loves you and wants you. You do not have to chase Ishmaels to get your Isaac. It is okay to wait on God. It is okay to be an outcast when you are living for God. It is okay to want good things and to wait for those good things. Go to school, obtain that degree, obtain another one, travel the world, serve God, get involved in ministry. Don't get so caught up in the idea of wanting a man that you stop living. Enjoy your youth and enjoy your *singleness. The man God has for you will help you achieve your visions and dreams. He will support you and lead you closer to Christ. I wish things could have been different, but you will survive to tell your story – a story that will save souls. So be proud of the older you that you will become!*

Beautifully made in the Image of God,
Jewlya

Nicole Norwood

Nicole, B.K.A. Nikki, she is a wife, mother, nana, daughter, granddaughter, aunt, niece, and cousin. Nicole's parents are Tony and Eva (Bee), and she holds her relationship with her family dear to her heart. She is married to Glenn Norwood, Jr; they are the parents of seven: Sean, Vandaro, BreAnna, Trey, Chris(Nicole), Isaiah, Elijah(Ambra). Grandparents to Zion, Genesis, Trey, and Sincere. She has two siblings: Anthony and Brittany.

Queen of Spades
~by Nicole Norwood~

Girl, you are M.A.D. Why are you mad? God has a funny way of handing us our cards. We don't get to pick them; we must accept the cards he gives us. It goes something like this…

"You're going to be born to these two individuals. You're going to look like them. You're going to talk like this. You're going to experience these things in your lifetime. And guess what?!? It may not be what you want or what you think you deserve, but here you go; it's how you were created. Here it is, this is your reality. Now how are you going deal with it?!?"

Good question… What do you do with the cards God gave you? The cards that won't change no matter who's in the game, who's got next, and don't even think about shuffling them to many times, because you get what you get. The game doesn't change. EVER! It's God's plan. It's God's game. Here you have it. These are your cards, and you're left to play your hand in this game called Life. How will you play? How will you win?

Don't fall victim to the game. I did! Here was my hand…Dark-skinned, wide-nosed, and as a bonus, a thick grade of hair (a cute way of saying nappy). Imagine with me! Looking back on things, today, I know these combinations of adjectives were good; they were beautiful; I'd even say unique. One day they would produce a woman who is confident in all areas of her life. When I was growing up, you could have NEVER gotten me to believe this. I did NOT want to be dark-skinned.

As far back as I can remember, I questioned why I was one of the darkest people in my family on both sides. I never got an answer that was "good enough". Early on through the years, I began to create my story based on the things I thought to be true. I started a collection of THE WORST of society's messages, people's words, and their actions. I accepted them as my truth and penned their narrative. As the saying goes, the most dangerous stories are the ones we tell ourselves.

A Dangerous Story

Even though I've never really been a mild or meek individual, people could easily mistake my demeanor as such. I thought that since I was a dark-skinned female, I HAD to deal with the looks, the NON-looks, and the way people treated me. I also thought I HAD to be loud and boisterous (some would call it ghetto) so that people will notice me.

I thought I HAD to always be with a crowd: the in-crowd, of course. I also thought I HAD to be in relationships with a particular type of guy to be noticed (oh yeah this is what they would have called being a fast-tailed Lil' girl). And as if that weren't enough, I thought I HAD to deal with the things people would say to me.

As a result, I made several (did I say several?) poor choices and poor decisions. I saw and acted on what "they" said; what they told me. And who were they?!? None of "them" were positive role models in my life, like my parents or my immediate family. They were all people who were nothing and meant absolutely nothing to me. Most of them I don't even associate with any longer. Others are those who now play the "victim," and lastly, there are those that I wish no ill will: the ones I am cordial with and keep it moving. Thinking back, I went through all of that for who...for what?

So often, people would tell me that I look mad and would ask me why. It was because I could not see the beauty past my skin tone when I looked in the mirror. I did not know that I was bound for greatness. I would think to myself that I was not mad; I was strong and confident. But the truth and the short of it is - I was M.A.D. I was a

Masterpiece And Didn't know it, and it showed! Ephesians 2:10 states that we are His workmanship (masterpiece). I am exclusive, having no equal, and created to be like none other.

News flash. I woke up and realized; I am a masterpiece, His masterpiece. Yes me! And so are you. God has determined our worth. The Bible tells me that I am fearfully and wonderfully made (Psalm 139). All I had to do was believe it and act according to what God said and what I now know to be true. I had to determine how I would see myself, treat myself, and expect others to treat me!

If I know and act worthy and pretty, people will treat me accordingly. Likewise, if I behave unworthy and ugly, I will be treated as such. At many points in my life, I've been a "pretty-ugly" person. Oh, how different this story could have been if I would have just focused on the right people and the right things, starting with me first.

REFLECTION

What statements have you made about yourself? Are they positive and encouraging or critical and doubtful? Why do many of us give so much value to other people and things that don't even matter? If someone asked you to name all the things you love, would any of those things be about you?

I've found that often, we usually don't include ourselves because it is "a natural," "implied," or we don't see ourselves to love ourselves. Kind of like I was when I was growing up. Words have power. You'd be surprised how it feels to affirm yourself! I encourage you to try it! Stop, right now, say something positive about you.

The Red Cards

I cannot tell you how many times I've heard that dark-skinned girls don't wear bright colors! For years, I did not wear bright colors because I am too dark. I thought that bright colors made me look darker; Lord knows that, as a young girl, I didn't want to look darker. There is one color that I despised. Red! Red was a deal-breaker, no matter what shade it came in. I was so adamant - NO RED! Let's talk about Red.

Red is a pretty intense color, bright and bold. I would not even dare to purchase anything red. Honestly, I did not start wearing red, comfortably or consistently, until I was in my late 30s. Because I didn't know what people would think, or even worse what they would say, I placed restrictions on the colors that I would wear. I would try on red clothing and attempt to step outside the box and would end-up playing it safe and going with the dark and uninteresting colors.

The dark colors helped me to blend in with the crowd. I guess I yearned to blend in since I told myself that being dark also meant being boring. Who makes up this stuff? And, who makes it up about themselves? Who started the saying that dark-skinned girls don't wear red? Why did I agree with them and convince myself that it was the truth?

I just knew if I wore red, I would stand out *in* the crowd, but little did I know I wanted to stand out. When I first began to wear red, people would quickly point out that they've never seen me wear red. To my surprise, I received several compliments, more than I could have ever imagined. Though I walked with my head held high and strutted boldly, I had to work hard to extinguish negative thoughts that would pop in my head. I wanted to stand out *from* the crowd. I wanted people to see me because people needed to see me.

Why? Because I'm something to be seen! There was absolutely no reason for me to feel like I needed to blend in or hide. Today, if anyone asked me if dark-skinned girls wear red, I'd say, "YES!! I do!" Because I am bold, I am chic, I am confident, I am different, I am elegant, and I am HOT! I wear red pants and dresses. I wear red shoes. I wear red shirts and blouses. I wear red blazers, and I wear my big RED heart! Oh, and I carry a red phone! Any more questions?" Bill

Blass said, "When in doubt, wear red." I no longer doubt my beauty or me. I want to be different. Like Maria Sharapova said, "If everyone is wearing black, I want to wear red."

REFLECTION
How often do you step out of the box? What's stopping you? What makes you stand out from the crowd?

Self-Abuse

If you are expecting a story of a horrible childhood full of neglect and abuse, sorry!! That is not my story. Because of my internal struggles and self-esteem challenges, someone might think my parents, or my family were emotionally, physically, or even verbally abusive towards or neglected me. That would not be the case; no hidden stories and no deep secrets. Both my parents were present and positive, and my immediate family was full of positive role models.

However, with my bad choices and the need to be accepted, even then, I was strong-willed and opinionated. I was raised right but chose to do wrong. This one was not on bad parenting, which shows us we can't always blame parents. If we are looking for someone to blame for our choices, we don't have to look far. We can look in the mirror and hold that person accountable. We can choose right from wrong.

Now that we have that out of the way: let me go into more about this thing called "self-abuse." I'm speaking metaphorically about allowing myself to be poorly treated, taken advantage of, and allowing others to "think" that they could do and say whatever, to me, whenever. In most cases, I would say I allowed this mainly from males.

As I reflect, I recall times where I dealt with it from some females as well. The truth is, I've even let some family members get away with it. I call it self-abuse because when I look back on the "why" of it all, the only reason I can think of is that I thought I was helping these people. I gave them the benefit of the doubt and thought they would change or that I could change them. THAT was THE farthest thing from the truth!

The crazy thing is that I could have snapped, effortlessly, and hurt people's feelings. But for whatever reason, I refrained, and this caused some to believe I didn't have it in me. In my younger years, I gave so much of my attention, my energy, my money, my peace, myself, my space, and my time to people that didn't deserve it or me. I gave those things and myself willingly. The sad part of it all is that I'll never get those things back.

Here is what I say to you about self-abuse, you teach people how to treat you. If it feels off, you better believe something is off. If you see something, don't let them persuade you that you didn't. If they said it, trust me, they meant what they said. If they did it once, they will, most likely, do it again...And again! If you give it, they will take it.

My uncle always told me that the best predictor of future behavior is past behavior. I found out the hard way that people are who they are. They will take advantage of you, if you allow them, and will do it as long as you let them. The keyword in self-abuse is self. Please, do not abuse yourself or sell yourself short on what you deserve. Remember, you are a masterpiece, and respect is required.

REFLECTION
Have you ever exposed yourself to some unnecessary drama? Have you put other people and their needs before your own? When will you decide that you are first and foremost in your life? Reminder, if you don't put yourself first, then who will?

Girls Just Want to Have Fun

A strong-willed, opinionated, tough girl who often presented herself to be the total opposite to preserve relationships, that girl was me. Yeah, that accurately sums up my young lady/young adult years. If I had to choose a song that would represent those years, it would be 'Girls Just Wanna Have Fun' by Cyndi Lauper. Remember, I thought to be dark-skinned was boring.

So, what do regular people do when they are bored? You know; the people who lead average lives; not a lot of fuss or hoopla; the people that do not need extras; the people who create excitement for themselves.

For the most part, I indulged in the most typical mischievous stuff. I skipped school, I drank (never smoked or did drugs), I vandalized, I fought, I cussed, I lied, and I talked back. To take it a step further, I went places I shouldn't have gone, did things I should never have done. As if I needed more excitement, I "dated" people that I shouldn't have dated!

Does this sound like anyone you know? Need I say more? While I was creating some excitement for myself, at the same time, I sacrificed some close relationships. I realize now that there was not that much excitement in the world that I should have given up what was important to me. I thank God for praying parents, grandparents, uncles, and aunts; without their prayers and care, I could be telling a different story. I survived my careless years of excitement, and God allowed it to become a testimony that I can use to aid my daughter, BreAnna, as she and others like her journeys towards womanhood.

The Rules of the Game

Growing up as an only child, to my mom, and the oldest of my paternal siblings, Anthony, and Brittany, I didn't have anyone in my immediate family who was my age to look up too. My parents were just that - PARENTS! They were teen parents.

My momma was 16, and my daddy was 17 when they had me: so, what in the world could they tell me? Sure, they could talk to me about life from a teenage perspective. As long as I didn't have a child as young as they did, I thought I was doing great.

Like most teen parents, mine had to grow up fast get it right early. Because they had to do it quick; fast and in a hurry, they had the blueprints. They knew they would not experience life as a typical teenager. They knew how hard it would be to create a life that a child would be proud to live. They knew that they would have to make sacrifices and that the road would not be easy! They gave me the directions, and I still did it my way. If I'd only listened to my parents, I could have saved myself a lot of trouble, headaches, and heartaches.

Plus, I owed it to them to represent them well. Even as teen parents, imperfect parents, I must admit they did a darn good job with me. Honestly, I learned a lot from them about what-to-do and what-not-to-do. Although I did not turn out bad, the road could have been much easier had I just watched a little closer, listened a little harder, and obeyed.

Like some children, I never totally ignored the lessons; I simply pushed them to the back of my mind for a while. Ok, a while ended up being years. My parents were doing their job by telling me what not to do, but as hard as they tried to keep me from going astray, I still did my own thing. I was not sheltered or forbade to be me.

Even though I was not perfect, I believe my parents would be surprised at some of the things I have done. My daddy used to tell me, "I will ALWAYS give you guidance; that'll never stop." I am grateful that they never gave up on me, even when I gave them reasons too. Instead, they let me live and learn. Little did I know, everything my parents were trying to tell me would come to pass and would eventually impact my adult life, especially my parenting skills.

As an adult, I look back over my life and see myself relying on their wisdom and advice. I also find myself sharing some of the lessons and conversations with my children:

reminding them that they may not understand it now, but, eventually, they will.

REFLECTION
Can you think of a time that you were given advice and decided that you would do it your way? How'd that work out for you? Have you ever had to tell someone "thank you" for the lessons? What are some life lessons you live by today?

The Game Changer

It's true sometimes it takes a significant event for a person to look at their lives and see that something must give. For me, it was having children and being a single parent to Sean and Vandaro. You would think that I would have gotten it the first time. It took me two tries!

Although I'd been in church all my life, while I was pregnant with my first son, at the age of 19, I decided to re-dedicate my life to Christ. I decided to re-dedicate because when I initially accepted Christ and was baptized, I was young and did not know all the details of what my decision meant.

This time, I felt it would be the best decision for me; to help me be a better parent for my unborn son. I was also hoping that it would help me influence others to be better people. Though it made a difference, what I was hoping for didn't happen. However, I became more aware and intentional about a lot of things. I recognized that I would have someone looking up to me. I was the first person and wanted to be the only person he had to look to as a guide for and throughout his life.

Ralph Waldo Emerson wrote, "Men are what their mothers made them." Having a child was a significant motivation for me to live better. It's one thing to take yourself through unnecessary situations, but when the decisions you make are conscious decisions that can negatively affect your children... HMMM!

Shortly after the birth of my first son, I sat and wrote him a poem. I often read and meditated over the words to internalize them and recharge myself to act on the words I wrote. As I began to navigate life as a single parent, it became more and more apparent that I had to break my vicious cycle. Did I? Not immediately. But my son NEVER was exposed to any my foolishness.

Trust me, being a single parent is far less humiliating than having your child see someone treating you badly. I made sure that he would always be able to see me in my purest form and the best light. I was hopeful that I would serve as a guide for him to make good choices when it came to women, and he would treat them accordingly.

Four years later, I birthed my second son. God entrusted me with two young men that I had to show the way. They needed to see a woman treated like a queen: so, when they grow up, they will treat women - their woman - as such. The bible tells us that children are a gift from God. God knew that my children would bring me closer to Him, and I did too.

Early into my motherhood, I decided that I would not bring any person around my children unless I felt they deserved it. They would have to have a long-standing place in my life. Guess what? I was able to stick to that decision, and it proved to be a significant step in the right direction. Was I the perfect mother? Probably not! Did I strive for perfection as a mother? Yes, every day! Although tough love can make this seem untrue, still today, my goal is to be a mother of perfection.

As a parent, I discovered a great scripture to strengthen me while raising my sons: Start children off on the way they should go, and even when they are old, they will not turn from it (Proverbs 22:6, NIV). Anyone who truly knows me knows that I am blessed; my sons are good children; they are my world. They will always hold a special place in my heart. They make me proud to embrace the title of "mama."

Although I would have never imagined (nor would I recommend) being an unmarried mother of two, I wouldn't change being a single mother for anything in the world. For me, motherhood became a game-changer!

REFLECTION
Have you experienced a significant event that changed you? Was the change Good, Bad, or Indifferent?

The Re-Deal

Once I was asked, "How'd you get all of this confidence?" I didn't even have to think about the answer as I laughed and shared, "Trust me, I haven't always been this way." It's funny how people sometimes think or say I have too much confidence! I smirk when I hear things like, "I'm *too strong for a female*, I'm *mean*, I *always* have to be right, I'm *controlling*, I'm *conceited*, I'm *too direct*," and the list goes on. Too much, huh? Maybe, but I'm not too much; I'm just not in the business of being a people pleaser anymore, and I'm not looking to be.

Keep in mind, some of these people have been around a long time, but most have not. Some of them and their opinions matter, but most do not. The truth is that today, I'm okay with being who I am! The same me who put others before me in the past is the same me who now puts me first. Oh, you liked the old me better? ! Well, this is the new me! I am her and she is me! I always had it in me, but in my immature years, many would not have been able to handle it. Trust and believe, a lot of people have been saved from all the parts of me! Now that I am mature, I have better control of my tongue and my actions. To not, is almost a losing game. If you're too docile, you lose; and if you're too bold, you lose. Being your authentic self in this game of life can be tricky. You might want to throw in your hand from time to time.

Don't confuse temporary circumstances as a permanent destination.

At times, you may feel like you have been dealt a losing hand or two but play smart. Don't confuse temporary circumstances as a permanent destination. You will make it; all is not lost. You must find balance, and it must be a healthy balance. The right balance of strength and frailty is essential! The right balance of faith, family, friends, and fun is necessary! The right balance of confidence, courage, resilience, intelligence, genuineness, and honesty is imperative! Yeah, I found it and I've found my winning hand. I'm winning! Like Jekalyn Carr says, "EVERYTHING attached to me wins!"

Winners Win | Inspired by my husband

Twenty-three years ago, I met a man that immediately said to me, "I don't date dark-skinned girls." REALLY!? DUDE!? GOD!? Here we go again. "I told myself, "Ok, cool. Well, that's not going to change anytime soon. As a matter of fact, I won't even call him." After about two weeks, we ended up on the phone - not sure who called who. But as it turned out, we would end up being good friends.

After a few years, and a roller-coaster friendship, we finally decided to engage in a different type of relationship. Though being friends, first, certainly helped, we still had lots of baggage. On top of that, we both brought children into the mix. Because we were best friends, we felt that the right move was to get married and blend our families. We probably could have used a few more years of prep, but that's neither here nor there. We quickly found out that family blending is not easy. When blending families, your children must know that there is always a place for them; that they have a voice. They need to know that they are "sharing" their parent as opposed to their parent being "taken away." They also need to *feel* the love early and often.

Although it wasn't easy, we have fun as a large family. We've had our share of issues, but our good times, as a couple and a family, have outweighed the bad times by leaps and bounds. We were determined to succeed. Most of our issues came from outside influences. We learned that we had to quickly separate ourselves from people who did not sow into us as a family.

Through it all, it was one of the best decisions that we made for all of us. (Clearing my throat) I think this is a perfect place to insert 'never say what you don't do.' Right husband?

Overall, this new hand dealt is a keeper; it's a winning hand. Overall, I see this new hand I've been dealt as a keeper. It's a wining hand. I am the proud wife of Glenn Norwood Jr. He is a man who has lots of similarities to my daddy. I am a proud mother of seven children; Sean, Vandaro, BreAnna, Glenn III "Trey," Chris (Nikki), Isaiah, and Elijah (Ambra), and I am Nana to Zion, Genesis, Trey, and Sincere. We refer to ourselves as the NORWOODCREW!

As Queen of the NORWOOD CREW, I go hard! I strive to be the best that I can be and seek to live Proverbs 31:28 (KJV) out loud, "Her children arise and call her blessed; her husband also, and he praises her." I can't help but hope that they are watching and listening to the good, the bad, and even the ugly.

Ultimately, deciphering what to use and what not to use in their adult lives. Most importantly, I hope they REMEMBER THE LESSONS.

REFLECTION
In what areas of your life are you winning? Are there areas that you could make some changes?

M.A.D.

Girl, you are a **M**asterpiece **A**nd **D**on't Know it. Why are you MAD? I'm MAD because I could have given my parents and family a bad rep, with some of my choices. I'm MAD because I took myself through some unnecessary mess! I'm MAD because I helped write a fake story and allowed some people to play main characters; I let them believe that they were stars in my life. I'm MAD because I didn't treat myself like the queen God created me to be and that I am. Therefore, neither did others.

It doesn't matter how the game begins; you determine how it ends.

I'm MAD because I wasted a lot of time on and with a lot of people. I'm MAD because when I should have let go, I didn't. I'm MAD because I allowed people to say things to me and about me, and I let it sidetrack me. I'm MAD because when people thought they were playing me; I didn't tell them I knew what they were doing. Yet, even without me checking and telling them, they would eventually play themselves. I'm MAD because, with some poor choices, I let some close relationships go wayward. Oh, wait, those aren't the real reasons I'm MAD...

Let me tell you why I'm M.A.D. I'm a **M**asterpiece **A**nd **D**isplay it. I have beautiful dark skin, and you can't tell me anything different. I have thick dark hair, thick lips and thick thighs, and high cheekbones. My faith is in God. Therefore, I let go, and I let God. I am a praying mother and wife; my husband is the bomb, my children are amazing to me, and my grandchildren are my inspiration, and I have been very much so blessed with a good career. I have a big heart, a great relationship with my parents, some genuine friends, and a healthy support system.

I speak with confidence and authority and always tell my truth; I don't care what others think or say as I don't seek anyone's approval. I don't do drama, and I live life loud with no regrets. I laugh, I cry, and I DO ME! Yep, I'm mad! I'm a **M**asterpiece, **A**nd **D**o Know it, and it shows!

The Lesson

It's easy to fall into the traps of the standards of the world. People will always have opinions, and society will have its say. It's very easy to self-criticize. The bottom line is your self-worth is all up to you! According to Gary Hendel, "I AM: Two most powerful words, for what you put after them shapes your reality." How you see yourself speaks volumes.

Speak life into yourself, and every dead situation, and watch what happens. I urge you to start a daily habit of affirming yourself. You matter! It doesn't matter how the game begins; you determine how it ends. You are your priority. Learn yourself and Love yourself.

Lessons from My Momma

Be there for your children; no matter what
Buy more than one of everything, you'll need it
Clean up and clean often
Do for your family when they need you
Don't have a lot of men in your house around your children;
don't let no man hit on you
Have a giving heart; if you experience a hardship, you'll get
through it
Keep your children safe at all cost
Make sure they have a relationship with their grandparents
Pay your bills and pay them on time; work hard for what you
want; you can always make something out of nothing; your
children come first

Lessons from My Daddy

Always give your children guidance, no matter how old they
are; be a good person; be resilient; be stress free; be there
for your children
Call people back
Clean, clean, and clean some more
Don't job hop; don't Quit-we are not quitters
Go to college/get a degree
Find a good man; relationships are important but keep a
small circle
Tough love is necessary; work hard and give it your all; your
children are your priority- no one else's

A Message to My Younger Me

Dear Younger Me,

Be the woman you needed as a girl. You will be born to young parents, Tony, and Bee, who you will grow with, and they will take great care of you. They will make a way to provide you with all that you need and even taking it a step further to give you most of the things you want. They will have their go-to-relatives, who will ensure that you are cared for whenever your parents are not available. Even at times when harm is near, they will never allow you to be in distress. Through their actions, they will show and teach you how to be a dedicated worker. They will be your teachers of life and will provide some tough love along the way. They will show you that even though they may not see eye to eye at all times, they can be civil with each other for your sake. Though they may not be perfect, they will give you all of them. They will show you that two families can blend and make it work. They will travel, eat, and party together. They will demonstrate and emphasize to you that your children are your world. They will be your parents first, and then your friend. Although your daddy will not live in your home, he will never be absent. He will show you what to look for in a man. You will be daddy's girl in every sense of the word. Love them always. You'll always be exposed to faith and attend church. You'll have good and bad experiences, but the good outweighs the bad. You'll spend a lot of time with your grandfather, who will always take great care of you. Your grandmother will be your angel in life. You'll have a close relationship with a few of your aunts and uncles; they will be like second moms and dads to you. You'll see some dysfunctional relationships and behavior. You may not understand all of it, but you'll look back and know the direction you do not want your life to go in. You'll be scared at times, but don't worry; your family is always one phone call away. At times you will wish that things were different but hang on; storms don't last forever. Your later years will be *fun. You'll make your own decisions, and you'll be able to discern even more the direction your life will go. You always do great in school. Of course, you'll get into mischief, though you'll always be a good girl. There will be a couple of people that you will be "in love" with, and through the years, you will find out that they were overrated. You'll also have fly-by-night-situationships that are just that. You'll have your cousins as your first friends. You'll meet good friends, though many of them won't be lifelong. You'll develop strong bonds with some; others will be fragile. Many of your relationships and friendships will be for a reason, and others will be only for a season. But there are a few that will come for a lifetime. You will attend and graduate college, but the traditional route was not an option. Since you chose to become a mama, you must travel the long road. You'll have to put the needs of your sons before yours until they are adults. As a single mom, navigating life for three, you'll strive to do right, and at times you will get it all wrong. You'll have to love some people enough to let them go so that you are not blocking your blessings. You will be just fine, although it may not seem that way. You'll possess unmatched intelligence and enjoy a successful career that affords you some life luxuries. Some people will call you "too good" or "conceited"; you know your goals and don't settle for anyone. You'll become a big sister and an auntie. You will become very important to your family and friends. You're headstrong and soft, wrapped up in one. You'll have a hard exterior, but on the inside, you are full of love, care, and concern. You will be wise for your years, sharing your wisdom will many people; some will hear you and others will not, share it anyway. You will go out of your way to help anyone who needs it. People and situations will frustrate you to no end but love them anyway. Having close relationships will be most important to you than ever. While life is good, and your independence unmeasured, you'll meet a praying man. Neither of you will have intentions of becoming serious in your friendship, but you'll become good friends and decide that there is more. Your children, and his, may have to adjust, but an adjustment is a good thing. In the end, they will appreciate the blend. You will marry him,* and you will raise a daughter who will look to you as her model on how to be a woman and sons and bonus sons who will seek to know how to treat a woman. Together you're stronger; you will be great examples of parenting and relationships with your children. They will make you proud. Things will get messy at times, and the road will not be easy, but your home will be full of faith, family, and fun, and you wouldn't have it any other way. Joshua 24:15(b) (KJV), "...but as for me and my household, we will serve the Lord." To be the woman you needed as a girl, you would have had to do many things differently. Yes, you would experience life for yourself, but you would have listened harder and chosen better relationships. You would have taken the road less traveled [Robert Frost], and not even looked twice at the crowded ones. You would have given a lot more consideration to those who came before you and the lessons they learned. Love yourself and let it be known. Have no regrets, and don't be resentful; everything happens for a reason. Continue to be a lifelong learner and continue to live out your values and stay committed to your faith. Be a leader, not a follower; be a mentor; be an example; be a great wife, provider, mother, and nana, and make your family proud. Be a good friend: a virtuous woman full of pure intentions. And, tame your tongue and have the right attitude during times of conflict. "Let all bitterness, and wrath, and anger, and clamor, and evil speaking, be put away from you, with all malice: and be ye kind one to another, tenderhearted, forgiving one another, even as God for Christ's sake hath forgiven you," Ephesians 4:31-32 (KJV). Be encouraged, brown girl, you are a queen. Take the rain and the pain; learn from them. Be your own you. Live your life loud and dance and sing like no one is watching. Shuffle the deck, take the hand that God dealt you, study your hand, make your best moves, and remember...

The "black" cards always win!!!

P.S. There is only one Nicole "Nikki " Renea Norwood and God loves her, and you will too!

Beautifully made in the Image of God,
Nikki

Author's Contact Information

Rachel Wright – Rmmgraphicdesigns@gmail.com

Angel Richardson – ajones107@comcast.net

Lauren Nowlin – laurennicolereigns@gmail.com

Lisa Bellamy – lisa.bellamy0911@gmail.com

Lauren Kelley – thenowlingroup@gmail.com

Pastor Desion Stewart – hm5ministry@gmail.com

Dr. Tuesday Tate – drtuesdaytate@gmail.com

Jewyla Payne – jyateman@yahoo.com

Nicole Norwood – ureigninc@gmail.com

About Executive Editor

~ Dr. Tuesday Tate ~

Dr. Tuesday Tate is the CEO of ATK Speakers and Publishing (ATKSP) Firm and the Executive Editor of the Publishing arm of the Firm. ATKSP Firm not only publishes collaborative and individual works, they also provide a 1-day Writer Workshop and a 3-day Speakers Training. The Firm is on target to train and equip professional speakers and writers and too publish several collaborative and independent authored works. ATKSP Firm seeks to equip clients in writing their best work, telling their story, speaking their truth, and readying them for their next.

ATK Publishing has released several collaborative works. Dr. Tuesday also has two independent works *"Waiting | Mastering the UnAvoidable"* and *"Grace Broken."* They can all be found on Amazon. She is also due to unveil *"My Daddy's Demons"* in 2021. It has been said her books are "tools for today and life... You will reference and come back to them year after year."

Dr. Tuesday is a multi-facet, progressive, and consummated professional as the CEO of both Vision Focus Group World Wide (providing Strategy and Certified Training and Coaching Services) and T. Tate Ministries International. She effectively uses her talents, gifts, skills, and knowledge as an ordained Prophetic Minister, Coach, television and radio personality, motivational speaker, author, publisher, and trainer to help individuals and organizations identify, document, and achieve their goal. She is charged and elated to be living her life's purpose and helping others do the same. To learn more about the woman, entrepreneur, minister, author, life and relationship advisor, media host, speaker, executive coach, and trainer, please visit her brand site at www.drtuesday.net, via Social Media, and YouTube at @DrTuesdayTate.

To learn more about Dr. Tuesday and to order her self published books and other ATKP Authors works, visit her brand site @ www.drtuesday.net.

Dr. Tuesday Tate

ATKSP Firm

8401 Moller Rd., Ste. 68244

Indianapolis, IN 46268

8889910979

atkspfirm@gmail.com

www.atkspf.com

Grace BROKEN
MY JOURNEY TO CONTENTMENT

TUESDAY TATE

This Is Who I Am

Now Open For Booking!

Check out her site and book her at www.drtuesday.net

Minister, Author, Publisher, Certified Trainer, Certified Coach (Executive and Relationship)

Certified Behavior Consultant, National Speaker (Motivational and Inspirational)

DrTTate · drtuesdaytate

JOIN DR. TUESDAY WEEKLY FOR

TUESDAYS WITH TUESDAY

4TH WATCH POWER PRAYER & TEACHING

FB Live @ 5am EST every Tuesday. Come ready to be equipped, empowered, inspired, and enlightened!
Follow us on TWITTER, PERISCOPE, INSTAGRAM, YOUTUBE, LINKEDIN: @drtuesdaytate
FACEBOOK: http://www.facebook.com/DrTTate WEBSITE: www.visionfocusgroup.com or www.drtuesday.net
#drtuesday #thevisionconsultant #nextlevelthinking #relationshipcoach #relationshipsrule

ATK SPEAKERS PRESENTS 3-DAY EPIC SPEAKERS TRAINING

3-Day in-depth training and equipping is open to 20 ready to grow and go aspiring speakers, presenters, and those seeking professional development.

TARGETED MODULES INCLUDE:
IMPROMPTU SPEECHES, FROM PULPIT TO PLATFORM, TYPES OF SPEECHES, POWER PRESENTER, NEXT LEVEL NETWORKING, BODY LANGUAGE, VOICE POWER, SPEAKING AS A BUSINESS, CONQUERING FEAR

ATTENDEES RECEIVE:
DOUBLE OCCUPANCY HOTEL STAY, HOTEL BREAKFAST, PEER SUPPORT, IMPROMPTU AND PREPARED SPEECH WITH CRITIQUE, VIRTUAL ACCESS TRAINING FOR THOSE UNABLE TO JOIN US ON-SITE, OPPORTUNITY TO JOIN THE ATK SPEAKERS FIRM

DR. TUESDAY TATE | WWW.ATKSPF.COM | DRTUESDAY.NET

ATK PUBLISHING PRESENTS 1-DAY EPIC WRITERS WORKSHOP

1-Day in-depth training is open to 20 aspiring independent, self-publishing, and or contributing authors

Training Includes:
Understanding self-publishing, marketing, edit proof, writing approach, know your voice, writing styles, blockers, barriers, burdens, self management, become an unapologetic writer

Dr. Tuesday Tate | atkpublishing@gmail.com
www.drtuesday.net | www.atkspf.com

DrTTate   drtuesdaytate

Made in the USA
Monee, IL
12 October 2021

79853498R10149